What people are sayi   T0042910

Mature Flâneur

From a Medieval village in suburban Paris to a summertime-only ski slope along the Highway to Hjelle — and multiple remarkable points beyond and between — *Mature Flâneur* is a slow-traveler's excursion through landscape, time, and the quintessentially human. Whimsical, unexpected, frequently revelatory, exquisitely observed (and written), this is vintage Tim Ward — I loved it.
Ian Weir, author of *The Death and Life of Strother Purcell*

In this wonderful book, Tim Ward invites us to slow down our lives enough to find the hidden gems right in our midst. Through his vivid accounts of his travels through Europe during his "senior gap year" with his wife, I could imagine meandering through the small lanes he discovered in Paris, felt my heart racing as he negotiated the vertiginous Dolomite hiking trails, and burst out laughing during his near-accident motorboating in the Arctic Circle. Tim Ward is a brilliant storyteller and we benefit from his indefatigable curiosity. Whether you decide to follow in his flâneuring footsteps or not, after reading this book you will see the world around you with different eyes.
Stephanie J. Miller, author *of Zero Waste Living, the 80/20 Way*

Tim Ward, a.k.a. the Mature Flâneur, has a special talent for noticing the little details of geography, architecture, food, history, wildlife, and culture. His vivid descriptions transported me to his side. From bustling cities filled with history to striking natural landscapes, this book offers a captivating journey through some gorgeous parts of northern and southern Europe.

For adventure, discovery and enlightenment, it's a true gem, not to be missed.
Bart W. Édes, author of *Learning from Tomorrow*

With rising awareness of the severe climate impacts of jet travel, perhaps you are thinking about flying less — or not at all. *Mature Flâneur* is the perfect solution: armchair travel at its best. But be careful, reading it may arouse your wanderlust!
Lawrence MacDonald, author of *Am I Too Old to Save the Planet? A Boomer's Guide to Climate Action*

If you have ever dreamed about strolling through the gardens of Paris, marveling at the glaciers of Norway, or exploring the back alleys of Lisbon, buy this fabulous book! Tim has an eye for detail and an adventurous spirit that brings every nook and cranny of Europe to life. Escape where you are through these charming pages and who knows, you may be inspired to book a European ramble for yourself.
Lisa Foster, author of *Bag Lady: How I Started a Business for a Greener World and Changed the Way America Shops*

With a keen eye for the telling detail, a sense of the absurd, and an underlying philosophy of life and traveling through it, Tim enthrals as he entertains. But a warning: reading him will make you long to flâneur too, as I was forced to do!
C.C. Humphreys, novelist and director of the rock-opera version of Tim's first book, *What the Buddha Never Taught*

I have been a Tim Ward fan since *What the Buddha Never Taught*. Whether he is exploring Buddhist temples in India, or discovering the surprising pleasure of grilled sardines in Portugal, Tim is alive and alert to every thought and sensation sparked by his travels. In *Mature Flâneur* he shows that it's possible to find a life partner of matching and opposing sensibilities, adding depth and spice to the journey.

Melanie Choukas-Bradley, author of *Finding Solace at Theodore Roosevelt Island*

Would you like to quit your job and travel the world with no itinerary, no destination, and a beautiful companion? Tim Ward did just that, and then wrote a book about it. Dive into these pages and share the meditative wanderings, humorous encounters, and high adventures as he strolls, explores, climbs, hikes and navigates his way across some of the most beautiful places in Europe. Each chapter offers a tantalizing vicarious journey.

Marsha Scarbrough, author of *Honey in the River*

Tim Ward's descriptive prose creates mental snapshots in my mind of distant places while also seeding myriad thoughts in reaction to his musings that seep into philosophy, art, the sacred... and best of all the mysterious. This book is an adventure into the unforeseen world that reminds us that there is still much unique about our species and that one cannot plan for the unexpected.

Neil Richardson, author of *Preparing for a World That Doesn't Exist—Yet*

Not only does Ward Tim have the ability to transport his readers to wherever he happens to be in each moment, his grasp of science, geology and history truly educates us. I always come away from his writing feeling like I have unlocked some wisdom.

Jillian Amatt, editor, *Globetrotters*

I loved Tim's Mature Flâneur stories. He takes us to places that we'd never heard of, describing not only the architecture, geography and wildlife, but also the history.

Adrienne Beaumont, editor, *Globetrotters*

It is always a joy to dive into Tim Ward's stories and escape the world for a moment. Tim always brings something unforeseen to his narratives; his adventures are as authentic as it gets.

Anne Bonfert, editor, *Globetrotters,* and author of *Mein Traum von Afrika beginnt in Ghana*

Mature Flâneur

Slow Travel Through Portugal, France, Italy and Norway

Mature Flâneur

Slow Travel Through Portugal, France, Italy and Norway

By Tim Ward

CHANGEMAKERS
BOOKS

Winchester, UK
Washington, USA

JOHN HUNT PUBLISHING

First published by Changemakers Books, 2024
Changemakers Books is an imprint of John Hunt Publishing Ltd., No. 3 East Street,
Alresford, Hampshire SO24 9EE, UK
office@jhpbooks.com
www.johnhuntpublishing.com
www.changemakers-books.com

For distributor details and how to order please visit the 'Ordering' section on our website.

Text copyright: Tim Ward 2023

ISBN: 978 1 80341 535 2
978 1 80341 563 5 (ebook)
Library of Congress Control Number: 2023936559

A CIP catalogue record for this book is available from the British Library.

Design: Lapiz Digital Services

UK: Printed and bound by CPI Group (UK) Ltd, Croydon, CR0 4YY
Printed in North America by CPI GPS partners

We operate a distinctive and ethical publishing philosophy in
all areas of our business, from our global network of authors to
production and worldwide distribution.

For Teresa

Contents

Preface

The French term *flâneur* was coined in the nineteenth century by poet Charles Baudelaire to describe a sort of gentleman who ambled the streets of Paris in order to fully immerse himself in the city, to appreciate the whole city as a work of art. In our time, the word has been revived to describe a new and distinct way of traveling, far beyond the city gates of Paris (and applies irrespective of gender or social status). Just as the slow food movement celebrates the opposite of fast food—preparing a meal in an unhurried way and then fully enjoying each bite and sip—so a flâneur celebrates slow travel, relishing each moment, without rushing from place to place like a tourist on a schedule.

My wife Teresa and I, both in our early sixties, came across the concept of a *flâneur* as we were preparing to uproot our post-Covid lives to live and travel for a year in Europe as "digital nomads." But the real purpose was to create some space for discovering who we might become in our retirement years. Neither of us wanted to just molder in place. But we had no road map for how to do what we wanted. Because flâneurs are affected, and ultimately transformed, by their encounters with the places where they wander, *mature flâneur* seemed a most apt description of our new identity.

One challenge was how to stay connected to our friends and family back home. As a young man in the 1980s, I had hitchhiked through Europe and wandered through Asia for extensive periods of time. I wrote long letters home to my parents, siblings and friends. This gave me the important sense of communication I needed to stave off loneliness. By putting my most vivid experiences into words, I believed I could share the journey and my own transformation with the people I loved. Indeed, those letters home became the basis for my three first literary travel books, and set me on a life-long career as an author. So, when Teresa and I departed for Europe to begin our flâneuring life, I knew I needed something similar. I already had a blog on Medium.com, and simply repurposed it under the name *Mature Flâneur*.

Fortunately, the impulse to stay connected was so strong that it felt effortless to post once or twice a week. My mailing list grew, and so did the blog's popularity. Several months in, many of my friends who had been following our adventures started asking, "When are you going to write a book about your flâneuring?"

The book in your hands is the answer to that question. Its chapters are adapted from the blogs, and they keep the letter-like format of the original posts in order to give readers the in-the-moment perspective with which they were written. The narrative is meant to be a journey that you can join us on—a journey in which none of us can see what's coming around the next corner.

Through these chapters, every now and then I hit upon a "flânuer lesson"—an insight about how to travel like a modern-day flâneur. These lessons are compiled in an appendix, specifically for readers who might want to do more than vicariously experience the journey. I hope this book inspires some of you, whatever your age, to pack your bags, hit the road, and discover who you might become if you follow the way of the flâneur.

Acknowledgements

Thanks first to Teresa Erickson, my spouse and co-flâneur. You are the love of my life. Teresa edited every chapter of *Mature Flâneur*, and contributed many of the better photos to this book.

Next, thanks to the editorial team at *Globetrotters* (https://medium.com/globetrotters). The chapters of this book first took shape on my Medium.com blog and about halfway through my flâneuring year, I discovered *Globetrotters*, the most popular (and in my view, best-curated) travel publication on Medium.com. Since then, their publication has regularly featured my *Mature Flâneur* stories. I appreciate the work of the five women who manage and edit the publication, and also cultivate a lively online travel-writing community: JoAnn Ryan (founder and editor in chief), Jill Amatt, Adrienne Beaumont, Anne Bonfert, and Michele Maize.

I wrote this blog to stay connected to my friends and family. Their interest in what I was doing in my post-Covid life as a *Mature Flâneur* are the reason this book exists. My blog-posts were a modern equivalent of letters home; I wrote very specifically with these friends in mind. Their emails, social media comments, claps and likes, and even spelling and grammar corrections kept me feeling close to them all, even while wandering far away. It warmed my heart. Thank you, all.

A special thanks to Stephanie J. Miller, who voluntarily proofread the entire text, and to my friend and neighbor in Paris, Tanguy Mendrisse, a professional artist-photographer who took my photo on our street one day, and allowed me to use it on the book's back cover. *Merci beaucoup!*

And finally, my thanks to the amazing production team at John Hunt Publishing: editorial manager Frank Smecker, copy editor Denise Smith, cover designer Nick Welsh, and the good folks at Lapiz Digital who designed the book's interior. These folks are the unsung heroes of the publishing industry. The book would no more exist without them than it would without me.

Part I

Lisbon and Southern Portugal

Novice Flâneur

Chapter 1

Why Flâneur?

Flâneur is one of those lovely, elusive French words that has no real equivalent in English. "To wander without purpose, observing society" captures only what it looks like on the surface. Comparisons with words such as *saunter, amble, loaf,* or *idle,* make the concept seem indulgent. As the French literary critic Sainte-Beuve explained it, to *flâne* "is the very opposite of doing nothing." Indeed, it is to give yourself the gift of time: permission to live an unstructured life, and by so doing, discover something about the world, and about yourself.

In our case, my wife Teresa and I feel compelled to discover something crucial about ourselves now that we are in our early sixties: Who are we becoming at this transitional stage in our lives? After 25 years together, we could keep working a few more years, then gradually slide into retirement in our own community, surrounded by our dear friends and family. But is there more? Is there someone else we could be if were we not so busy being who we are? We knew we needed to create some empty space if we wanted to find satisfying answers to these questions.

Fortunately, we both love to travel. We fell in love while wandering the streets of New Orleans together. Later we developed a communications training business that involved a lot of international travel, and we found ourselves strolling through cities in over fifty countries through our long, joint career.

When the pandemic hit, our business collapsed. Our lives, like everyone else's, became confined to smaller spaces. Eventually we turned our workshops into webinars, and our training business recovered somewhat. Still, demand for our services shrank, and by spring of 2021 we knew we needed to reassess our future. Could we survive if we stopped work altogether? Our financial planner ran several thousand "Monte Carlo" simulations, and declared we were 99% likely to have enough to win—defined as dying before the money runs out.

As soon as vaccinations made travel possible again, we made the decision to pack up and leave the US for a year, inspired in part by our friend Stephanie, who departed her high-powered job at the World Bank to take a "gap year" which eventually led to her radically reinventing herself as a champion of the Zero Waste Movement, writing a book and founding her own business, Zero Waste in D.C. She never looked back. Could we do something similar? Take a "senior gap year" to flâneur around Europe and perhaps discover something new about ourselves?

We gave ourselves six months to pack up, terminate our lease in our suburban condo, and say our goodbyes. We sloughed off a lot of stuff, gave away furniture and boxes of dishes, lamps, artwork and books to family, friends and the local charity shop. Then, unburdened, we headed for Portugal—still mild and sunny in mid October. It was important not to plan this like a vacation. We booked a hotel for a week in Lisbon, but beyond that, we were determined to be spontaneous, and figure it out one stop at a time.

October 19, 2021, early in the morning, we arrived at the 400-year-old Hotel Janelas Verdes—meaning "Green Windows." They have a lovely breakfast courtyard where the entire walls are green, covered floor to roof with massive creeping fig vines, thick as my arm, and dotted with hundreds of unripened figs (sadly inedible) the size of lemons. We ate breakfast, went to bed, and slept through the day until dinner. Plenty of time, tomorrow, to begin our new careers as flâneurs.

Teresa and Tim newly arrived in Lisbon: ready for some empty space.

Chapter 2

Bedazzled by Azulejos

I'm knocked out by Lisbon. More than anything else, I'm stunned by the innumeral polished-tile buildings. These *azulejos* are everywhere. Even in some rather shabby backstreets in the Alfama—the heart of the old city—you see walls bursting with blue and white patterns, floor to rooftop. More rarely, dark cherry reds, muted orange-and-black, emerald greens, a vibrant turqoise, stark black-and-whites. They cover the fronts of ordinary houses, palaces, churches, subway stations, staircase walls, and yes, even bathrooms (the only place one is likely to find a tiled wall in the US).

This art form was brought to Europe by the Moors, who occupied Portugal and much of Spain through the Middle Ages. The name comes from Arabic, *al zuaycha*, which means "polished stone." That's why they origainlly featured geometric or floral patterns, not images of people and animals, long banned in Islamic art. Arab architects used polished tiles for design and practicality, as they reflect sunlight, and keep buildings cool under the hot sun.

In Portugal, azulejos did not become a public art form until King Manuel I visited Seville in 1503 and started to import the tiles home to decorate palaces and churches. They caught on like crazy in Lisbon. No whimsical passing fad, the passion for azulejos has persisted for more than 500 years. Decorating with azulejos became more popular in Portugal than anywhere else in Europe.

By the seventeenth century, religious panels depicted Jesus and the saints, and panoramas from the Bible filled the churches. Meanwhile, royals and nobles found new themes of

**A flâneur walks past one of Lisbon's many
azulejos-covered buildings.**

their own. Palace walls were decorated with vivid scenes of frolicking wildlife, hunting and seafaring. In one magnificent instance in the king's palace, the entire coastline of Lisbon was recreated in azulejos, a panorama that stretches over seventy feet (below):

Measuring nearly 23 meters in length, the Grand Panorama of Lisbon depicts 14 kilometers of the city, including palaces, churches, convents and ordinary homes just before the 1755 earthquake.

The eighteenth century industrialised the azulejos industry, and in the wake of the calamitous Lisbon earthquake of 1755, people rebuilt the city with tiles. Why? Because they had become a cheap and plentiful form of decoration. No way the citizens of Lisbon were going to just rebuild their homes and public spaces without beautifying them at the same time!

Lisbon Panorama

That obsession continues to this day: in subway stations, art galleries, the façades of modern office buildings, not to mention all the private interior spaces, including the courtyard of our hotel where an azulejos-backed fountain reveals a dozen playful monkeys.

Teresa tells me her parents, who lived in Lisbon when she was a child, used to carry boxes of azulejos back to the US every time they visited the old country. Her father tiled their walls, tables, contertops, backsplashes, even their porch. As Teresa so aptly told me, azulejos are "an unmistakeable expression of the Portuguese soul, a love of art that reaches into our hearts."

Though azulejos are everywhere, what seems most weird to me is that I have absolutely no memory of them from my previous visit to Lisbon 18 years ago when Teresa and I were there for a week. I can't explain it. This week the azulejos are jumping off the walls at me. Perhaps this is because my adult son Josh and I have been playing the board game Azul when I visit him in Philly. It's a pattern-making game based on, duh, azulejos.

Monkeys cavort in the garden of Hotel Janelas Verde.

This lack of memory is jarring, and makes me take stock of my general lack of awareness of my surroundings. Teresa will certainly tell you I'm a hunter more than a gatherer. If I am searching for something, I will usually find it. But if it's not on my map, I might not see it at all. It's not that I'm oblivious (I tell myself), just too focused to notice anything I'm not already looking for.

Flâneurs, however, "not only observe the details of city life as they saunter the streets. They are also" — so *Wikipedia* asserts — "affected by the architecture, indirectly and (usually) unintentionally affected by a particular design they experience only in passing." Walter Benjamin's book *The Paris of the Second Empire in Baudelaire* devotes one of three sections to the flâneur, "looking at the ways in which the architectural changes and shifts in urban planning in Paris during the 19th century interact with and reflect the evolution of modernist perceptions."

So, what does that mean for me, as I wander Lisbon, bedazzled by azulejos? One thing is for sure, they are opening my eyes to the beauty that surrounds me. Maybe something about the soul of this city is slowly starting to sink in.

Chapter 3

Suddenly I Like Sardines

Flâneur Lesson #1: Surprise yourself

I never really liked sardines, a Portuguese favorite. Fishy, oily, smelly, packed in a tin can for lord knows how long. Ugh. Teresa, however, always had a fondness for them. Not only is she Portuguese, her birthday falls on the national holiday of St. Antonio (June 13). It's celebrated in her hometown of Lisbon by people lighting bonfires in the streets and grilling—you guessed it—sardines. In fact, Teresa's mother says she went into labor after jumping over one of these bonfires. It was an age old custom for good luck. People actually call the holiday the *The Festival of Sardines*. Revellers stay up all night, drinking, dancing, leaping over the bonfires, and *feasting* on sardines— *feasting*! The blog *BePortugal.com* authoratively opines that "the Portuguese consume about 13 sardines per second during the St. Anthony celebrations."

How did the tiny fish become associated with the patron saint of Lisbon (who was born and raised in the city before moving to Italy)? One of Saint Antonio's miracles is called "The Sermon to the Fishes." According to the saint's hagiography, he was trying to deliver a sermon to a bunch of Italian heretics in the coastal town of Rimini, but they were not paying attention. In a fury, Saint Antonio declared he would be better off preaching to the fishes. At that moment, thousands of fishes—many of them sardines—rose to the surface, their heads up out of the water bobbing and looking at him attentively. The saint began to preach to his new audience, much to the amazement of the local townspeople, who shared the story of this miracle. Seven

15

centuries later, the Sermon to the Fishes is commemorated in the streets of Lisbon with the Festival of Sardines.

Despite the miracle, the festival hoopola, and Teresa's personal devotion, I remained a sardine skeptic. Then, our very first day in Lisbon, what did Teresa do? She dragged me to a sardine store called *Miss Can*. Yes, there are stores in Portugal that only sell canned sardines.

We took our seats at one of their three tiny tables, and together with our tins of sardines also ordered a side salad and glasses of wine. The waiter was also the proprietor of Miss Can, as well as the son of the founder. An innovator of different ways to flavour sardines, he waxed eloquent about the family business. Truly, his was a life-long passion, maybe even an obsession.

Reluctantly, a bite of the tinned fish. It tasted... not bad. Piquante, with olive oil and cayenne. Before we exited, we bought some extra tins for the road. Okay, I rationalized. Someone has figured out how to disguise the disgusting taste of sardines enough that they are edible.

Then, the very next day at a restaurant I saw grilled sardines on the menu. Much to Teresa's—and my—surprise. I ordered them. Grilled. No sauce to disguise them. Just the way Lisbonites eat them at the festival, with a drizzle of lemon juice. I nibbled. Light, yet firm. Not fishy, not oily, just tangy. The charcoal grilling seemed to have worked some alchemical magic in my mouth. Damn it, these are *delectable!* I thought. I finished the whole plate. Next thing you know, I was literally ordering grilled sardines every time we went out for dinner. If I smelled them cooking in the street, I got *hungry* for sardines.

I did a little online research. It turns out, sardines are good for you. They are loaded with antioxidants and essential minerals like copper. They prevent heart disease, macular degeneration, help fight cancer, improve brain function and bone health, combat anxiety and depression. Sardines have a low ecological footprint because they are low on the food chain; they eat plankton. Because of this, they are also less contaminated with mercury than fish higher up the food chain, like tuna.

I felt like one of St. Antony's heretics. Chastised and humbled, I now believe. Bring on the tasty little fishes!

Teresa was mightily bemused by my full-throttle conversion. She told me, "I'd like to think that in my lifetime I was able to accomplish a successful religious conversion, even if it's to the cult of sardines."

Of course, this little epistle is not only about sardines. It's about becoming open to things you always thought you didn't like. You might surprise yourself. And so I leave you with this question, dear brothers and sisters: "Do you like sardines— today?"

Chapter 4

The Flâneur Defeats the Digital Nomad

Flâneur lesson #2: Let go of work

Less than a week into our flâneuring life I received an email from a long-time client of ours inviting us to submit a "Request for Quotation" for exactly the kind of communications webinars Teresa and I deliver and planned to keep delivering, occasionally, to help pay expenses on the road. Although we were devoting ourselves to ambling through the colorful streets of Lisbon, I began sorting through the "RFQ" on my computer and launched into the process of completing the technical proposal forms that are required for this sort of thing.

While beetling away at it, I was aware that we had promised ourselves that though, yes, we wanted to keep delivering our virtual workshops, we were not going to do RFQs. Not only are they tedious, there is no guarantee that we would be the winning bidders. We had discussed only working with clients who want to work particularly with us for the quality we deliver, rather than a generic provider for a generic course.

Still, the income would be good, I told myself. It's the kind of work we do well, and for a client with a great mission we believe in. So I picked away at the technical proposal, a bit at a time, like a child picking at their Brussels sprouts.

Then my best friend, Jim, and his friend Meredith flew from Boston to Lisbon. Before we left the US they asked if they could join us for ten days. We threw our arms open and said yes! Part of flâneuring is saying yes to the unexpected. But honestly, there are very few people I would have welcomed into this early stage of our new life as much as Jim. He's been my best friend all my adult life. We met in our early twenties in a Buddhist monastery in Thailand, where we both stayed for several weeks, learning the ways of the monks. He was like an old war buddy, or perhaps prison cell mate might be a better comparison—we had served time together.

The four of us sauntered through Lisbon for two days—museums, restaurants, Fado bars. Then we took off in a white Jeep Cherokee rental, bound for the tiny beach village of Comporta. We headed south down the coast along a forested mountain road that zigzaged high above the sea with vertigo-inducing views. The road dropped to the remote Penedo Beach where we stopped. The beach rimmed the azure ocean like a crescent moon against a twilight sky. We wandered through Roman ruins that stood on a rocky outcrop above the bay—the foundations of a first-century sardine and salt processing center. Clearly, the Portuguese have been crazy about sardines for a long time.

Because we lingered at the fishy ruins, we missed the ferry at Setubal by five minutes. *De nada!* It's nothing! Plan B was to drive around the Estuario do Sado, and if it took another hour, so what? We sped through a forest of umbrella pines, with large drooping limbs spread out like, well, you guessed it. Next we passed miles and miles of cork trees—a major Portuguese industry. Stripped of their bark, their exposed trunks were chipotle red, as if deeply embarrassed by their involuntary nakedness.

Eventually we arrived at our destination, the tiny seaside village of Comporta. Thirty years ago, a younger Teresa had walked the empty beaches beyond the rice paddies and dunes. Back then, white sand stretched in either direction, not a structure in sight as as far as her eyes could see. Since then, the millionaire banker Ricardo Salgado bought a huge parcel of land in Comporta. While preserving much of the wilderness, others began building luxury bungalows in the area. Just enough development to support a local economy and sustain several decent restaurants, shops, and a handful of bars and cafés clustered by the beach parking lot.

Teresa rented one of the bungalows for the four of us for three nights. The development was surrounded by pines, with trees in each yard to break up the sunshine. Inside, it was spacious yet homey, deliciously cool as evening approached. The four of us settled in with a round of G&Ts, then we organized a simple dinner of salad, sardines, and *vinho verde* wine. Using a handful of dried pinecones, Jim lit a fire in the fireplace. In the flame's cosy glow, we drowsily relived the day's adventures.

Suddenly I recalled the RFQ was due at 9 a.m. the next morning. This was not going to get done unless I woke up at six. I shared my predicament with my comrades.

"Well, how does the thought of letting it go make you feel?" Teresa asked. I exhaled a deep, relaxing sigh.

The flâneur had defeated the digital nomad.

Chapter 5

Zambujeira Cliff Walks

Flâneur lesson #3: Put away your phone

The sand beach of Comporta runs twenty kilometers to the south. Beyond, for a hundred kilometers or so, the rocky Atlantic coast of Portugal rises up against the sea as high and dramatic as any cliffs you will find on the wild western shores of Ireland or Scotland. The wind blows furiously and the waves smash against the sheer black, yellow and red walls, digging deep caves and sculpting fantastical shapes, like some never-ending offshore art museum all along the coast.

Teresa and I, together with Jim and Meredith, spent three days at Zambujeira do Mar, a tiny fishing village that has become a well-shared secret for its pretty little beaches wedged in between

Zambujeira cliffs

the cliffs. We stayed at an old farmstead on the outskirts of the village that had been converted into an immaculate tourist hotel. The owners of Herdade do Touril maintained traditional elements—whitewashed walls, lavender trim, a giant fireplace in the common room. They had a huge farm-to-table vegetable garden out back, as well as sheep, goats, and a pair of hee-hawing donkeys in the field behind us that woke us up every morning. But, the heated saltwater pool and stylish restaurant/bar were probably not part of the original peasants' farm.

One morning we followed the cliff trail known as the *Rota Vicente*, or "Fishermen's Trail." The whole route runs the length of the cliff-coast, 226 kilometers in all. It's basically an eco-lover's version of the Camino Trail. Many people walk the whole length of it, with thirteen rest stops at fishing villages along the way. According to *Conde Nast Traveler Magazine*, it's one of the six most beautiful coastal trails in the world. Yet, we did not cross paths with many trekkers that sunny late-October morning, only one sizeable group of 20 or so Dutch hikers, plus a Canadian woman named Michelle in her early sixties who was doing the entire trail on her own. We met her again at lunch. She told us she was in search of a Frenchman who would marry her, so she could move to France. We were, of course, more than a thousand kilometers south of France... perhaps she was looking on the wrong trail?

With so much to do—the cliffs, the pool, grilled sardines, quaint fishing villages to explore, it felt sometimes that the flâneur was getting edged out by the tourist. But one morning, I found myself alone before breakfast. I brought my computer to the outdoor dining area, intending to tap away at the keys until they opened for coffee.

I sat facing a flowering bougainvillea that covered the terrace, a shower of pink blossoms on the ground next to it. After just a few seconds, I had the impulse to take pictures with my phone.

Hand in pocket, I stopped myself. Was I even really seeing the flowers? Was I going to take a picture so that I could look at the flowers later? When we click a photo, don't we mentally move on to the next thing? As if we are speed-dating reality, like constantly swiping left on some dating app? Instead of click and move on, why not just hang out with whatever strikes us as beautiful, then later, remember the feeling? So, I kept my phone in my pocket, settled in and just enjoyed the flowers.

Chapter 6

Learning to See

Flâneur lesson #4: Open your eyes

For the first week after Teresa and I arrived in Portugal, every night I would fall asleep quickly, then wake up a few hours later and lie awake for half the night. I cycled through various problems, items on my to-do list, political issues in the news, climate change. I knew none of these would be resolved while I was lying in the dark, but I could not seem to turn off my mind. I chastised myself: this is not the sleep of a flâneur, one who wanders about without a care. It's not even the sleep of the man I used to be, back in the US. It's the broken sleep of a man between two worlds.

My mind was still stressed, searching for problems to glom onto. I told myself, "Let it go. You can't solve it in bed." Then the next item in the queue popped up in its place.

What I'm coming to terms with is how much of my previous life was engaged in doing, rather than being. Even during the pandemic, when Teresa and I had long periods in lockdown with little work on our plate, the pandemic itself intensified my highly-focused mind. Just going grocery shopping was like running the gauntlet. For much of 2020, I would wear mask and gloves, and on returning home, we would wipe and wash each box of pasta, each piece of fruit, before putting it away. Then I would have a shower as if the air outside our condo was radioactive. I threw myself into my publishing work with a sense of urgency. In under 18 months, I put out two series of over twenty books on subjects related to resilience and visionary ideas for resetting our global future. Engaging with dozens of brilliant authors kept me motivated and my mind in high gear, as did the webinars Teresa and I developed and taught together, helping envirnoment and development professionals communicate better in this brave new virtual world.

I think since arriving in Portugal I have been experiencing something akin to velocitization: the experience of driving at high speeds on a highway for such a long time that when you take an off-ramp, you tend to exceed the local speed limit. To be a flâneur is to go slow. But I have not gone slow, mentally, in a long time. And so the world passes by in a blur.

In a previous chapter I wrote about the azulejos-covered walls on the streets of Lisbon, how the colorful, patterned tiles bedazzled me. It's as if the city is flashing me kaleidescopic warning signs I should attend to: "Go slow!" "look both ways!" And sometimes, that means look up... for example, on a Lisbon back street, I looked up and saw dozens of brassieres gaily flapping about as if they were Christmas decorations (below).

A week or so later in Comporta, Teresa, Meredith, Jim and I went grocery shopping together in the local market. I was diligently scanning the cereal shelves for something gluten-free I could eat (this is not a trendy preference; I have celiac disease). Jim came up to me, and asked where was my cart, so he could add something to it.

"I don't have a cart," I told him.

"Teresa said you do."

"I *never* had a cart."

He left, then came back a minute later. I had found some gluten-free oatmeal by then.

"Teresa says you *definitely* have a cart."

"No, I *never* had a... oh, wait, there it is!"

My cart was about six feet down the aisle from me, half filled with the items Teresa and I had picked out together no more than ten minutes earlier.

Fancy brassieres decorate a street in Real Principe, Lisbon. We have no idea why.

"Should I be worried about you, Tim?" Jim asked.

Well, this was the joke for the rest of the day. Honestly, it was a little scary. This was more than just a hunter mindset. Had I been so focused on stalking gluten-free oats, that I blanked out everything else?

A few days later, watching the sky over the sea in Zambujeira go from orange to pink to magenta, I was suddenly aware of a feeling in my chest like a slacking of the ropes, a subtle relaxation. With it came an awareness of how little I am still taking in of my experience. And wanting more of this. To observe without searching. To feel without an agenda. To breathe and let go.

The following week Teresa and I returned to the Lisbon area and settled into a rental apartment in Sintra for a week. I took a walk to the celebrated Pena Palace on the nearby mountaintop. It's more uphill than Teresa cared for, and she has seen the palace several times before, including during our previous trip to Portugal in 2003. Jim and Meredith had flown back to the US, so I found myself on my own, climbing toward that fanciful, exuberant castle in the sky. Late afternoon, it was still pretty crowded. Impossible not to notice that everyone, *everyone*, was either taking pictures with their phone, or posting the pictures they had just taken with their phones. Many couples looked as if they were on a professional photo shoot. Mostly the guys were taking photos of their girlfriends, who would then rush over to check the shots. Several of these women were dressed like fashion models, with flashy skirts and fancy shoes, despite the steep uphill hike from the parking lot.

I resisted the urge. I remembered that earlier moment in Zambujeira by the bougainvillea, and kept my phone in my pocket until after I took a good look around. I know this sounds strange, but it was also important for me not to make it a thing for myself that I was not taking pictures. Nothing to prove here. I just wanted to feel and enjoy, not click away as if I'm nothing but an extension of my device, a walking content provider for the Internet.

The Pena Palace is painted in bright reds and yellows, with whole walls tiled in blue-patterned azulejos, as if Van Gogh had swirled the bold primary colors of his brushes over it all. It's a crazy conglomeration of turrets and domes, Islamic arches and crenelated, curvy walls. There's even a fancy drawbridge that probably has never be drawn. When we visited in 2003, I recalled, we only saw the outside of the palace, to avoid the crowds (and the expensive ticket).

This time, I wanted to take my time and enjoy the sumptous interior rooms where the last kings and queens of Portugal once spent their summers: the glittering chandeliers; the rich red velvet bedspread in the queen's bedroom; the gleaming copper pots that covered the back wall of the giant kitchen. The stark, white-washed Stag Room, ringed with curving black antlers all round the walls. The cavorting nymphs and fauns, hand-painted on the wall of the king's study by King Calros II himself. The central interior courtyard held a dazzling array of so many different patterned azulejos, I could have sat and stared at them till nightfall. The tiles glinted blue and emerald green in the afternoon sun like so many glittering gems. I did take pictures, then. But not until I had soaked the colors in with my own eyes.

When I returned to our guest house at dusk, eyes full, feet weary, I shared my journey with Teresa, bursting with the new sights I had seen.

"I remembered we only saw the outside of the palace last time. It was amazing this, time, to see everything inside..."

"Oh, we did that," my love replied. "You and I saw the whole inside of the Pena Palace last time we were here."

The Pena Palace: what you see when you look up from your phone.

Chapter 7

Colares: Portugal's Tough Little Wine

"When examiners test new sommeliers, if they really want to throw them, they give them Colares wine. Usually, they can't even tell it's from Portugal! It tastes so unique, like nothing else."

Teresa and I nodded as Francisco Figueiredos spoke. He is the chief winemaker for Adega Regional de Colares, a cooperative winery for some 25 winegrowers in the Colares Region just west of Lisbon, between the hills of Sintra and the cliffs of Cabo de Boca—the westernmost point of mainland Europe. It is well off the beaten tourist track. In fact, no main roads will take you there. We were inside the co-op's vast, dark warehouse, lined with large wine casks, some blackened with age. The three of us stood alone around an upturned wine barrel, set with wine glasses, candles, and two slender 500 mm bottles, one red, one white.

We waited with anticipation for Francisco to pour.

During our tour of the winery, Franscisco had explained that Colares is the smallest wine region in Portugal, with just 26 hectares under cultivation today. It's also one of the most remarkable in Europe. The grapes are grown in the sand near the cliffs of the Atlantic coast. Of course, grapes can't actually grow in sand, so deep trenches have to be dug down to the ochre-yellow clay, 2–3 meters below the surface. Then, as the vines grow, the trenches are filled in with sand, until the trunk of the vine is level with the surrounding ground.

The vines' hardships continue at the surface. Frequent mists reduce the sunlight grapevines need, and the north wind blows so hard and so cool even in summer that the vines can't be elevated on trellises as in normal vineyards. Instead, the grapes grow low to the ground, sheltered from the wind. Since the sand holds in the sun's warmth, it insulates the buried trunks of the vines, and warms the grapes as they ripen on the surface.

This unique method of cultivation is the key to the grape's miraculous survival of the phylloxera epidemic that devastated Europe's vinyards in the late 1800s. Phylloxera is an aphid that feeds on the roots of grape vines, killing them. When the tiny pests arrived in Europe from America, they spread like a plague, ravaging the vineyards. Fortunately, wine growers figured out that they could graft European grapevines onto American roots. Because the American grapes co-existed with the aphids for a long time, the roots had a natural resistance, and so European wine was saved. To this day, all European grapes are grafted onto American roots.

Except wines from Colares. Why did the Colares grapes survive intact? Francisco explained: "The phylloxera tunnel through the ground to reach the roots of the vine. But they can't make a tunnel through sand; it simply collapses." So the laborious process which makes wine growing possible in this difficult region is what saved the Colares grape.

Sadly, Francisco continued, what really damaged the Colares region was uncontrolled property development in the 1980s, when thousands of summer homes and resorts were constructed along this wild coast so close to Lisbon. Only 15% of the original Colares vineyards remains. The good news is, that's up from a low of 14 hectares in the late 1990s. Today the region is part of a national park, protecting it from further development. Francisco tells us Colares city hall is also working on an application to UNESCO to declare the vineyards a World Heritage Site.

What makes the wine taste so special? The roots grow up to eight meters deep in the clay, sucking up minerals from the soil. And the cool wind and mist slows the pace at which the grapes ripen, so they are harvested later in the season. The result is a wine with a high acid content, lots of tannins, and next to no sugar. All this allows a lot of complexity, with flavor combinations you don't often find in wine.

First we tried the white. It hit me with lemon, but light, like a lemon blossom. That's the acid coming through, Francisco said. Teresa picked up herbal and mineral essences. It was light like Portgual's famous *vinho verde*, but very, very dry, which is what we both liked.

"Wild cherry," Francisco suggested as we tasted the red. Wow, he was right. I've never tasted so much cherry from a grape. It was surprisingly light bodied, but with leathery, woody tones coming through that you wouldn't expect could be held in a wine so light (with a bit of research, I discovered this was due to the extra thick skins on this hearty grape). As the wine warmed in our mouths, it revealed new, earthy flavors. Mushroomy, but in a good way. Clearly, this is a wine with a long story to tell.

Left to Right: Tom, Teresa, Paula and Tim sample a Colares red.

In order to absorb the wine's story thoroughly, we bought a few bottles to take with us to our next stop in Nice, France, to share with friends for Thanksgiving. Happily, we found out we can also order Colares wine online, and that the co-op ships to anywhere in the world. (Here's their website: www.arcolares. com)

To me, Colares wine brings to mind some of the things I have come to appreciate about the Portuguese in the month I have now spent in their country:

- Able to flourish in the midst of hardship
- Innovative problem-solvers
- Little, yet punching well above their weight
- Retaining their unabashedly unique characteristics in an increasingly homogenised world

Chapter 8

A Shrine to the Other Maria

Fado is Portuguese "Blues" music born in the slums of Lisbon in the 1820s. The word *fado* means "fate" or "destiny," and indeed, Fado songs are most often about love lost, separation, or chances for happiness missed. At the heart of Fado is the emotion *saudade,* a Portuguese word that every online site says defies translation into English. Teresa, who was also born in Lisbon, says that "longing" comes the closest.

"It's not nostalgia, though," she tells me. "Not simple sadness in the face of loss. It's a deep, deep feeling you have connecting

Fadista Ana Margarita performs on stage in Porto. She told her audience it did not matter if we did not understand Portuguese: her heart would sing directly to our hearts.

you to what you long for, and that can be anything: a lost friend or lover, a place, a dream for your future."

To our surprise, flâneuring through the winding streets of the Mouraria in the oldest part of Lisbon, Teresa and I discovered the actual birthplace of the woman whose music marked the emergence of Fado from the shadows into the light.

The plan for the day, in as much as there was one, was to start at the Chapel of Our Lady of Health, wander through the backways until we got hungry, and then find our way to *Zé da Mouraria,* a traditional Portuguese restaurant that Teresa particularly wanted to try. The chapel was built as an appeal to the Virgin Mary for her to intercede with God and save the city from the plague, which ravaged Lisbon during the sixteenth century. The crowned statue of Mary at the front of the chapel is still paraded around the neighborhood once each year in thanks for her deliverance.

Just behind the church, the narrow streets zigzag up and along the hillside towards Sao Jorge Castle through the *Mouraria,* one of the few parts of the city that survived the earthquake of 1755. The name means "Moor-area." It's the old quarter of the city where the muslims were confined after the Christian reconquest of Lisbon in 1147. Because of its winding alleyways and crooked streets, the Mouraria remained a magnet for outcasts. It attracted a rougher crowd of immigrants, sailors and sex-workers. Now it's just starting to emerge as a rather hip part of Lisbon, while still keeping its authentic character.

We wandered around until our feet got sore, then headed in the general direction of the restaurant. The road narrowed, then widened into a tiny square with two trees loaded with oranges in the center. The houses here were old, not more than two stories, with some of the doors laughably tiny. The plaster walls were cracked, showing through to brick, and the paint chipped and faded. But whimsical artwork decorated the square: a metal whale, a portrait of an old woman as if she were looking out of a window. A fresco of a woman singer, wearing a shawl and black dress, holding a guitar, dressed from an age gone by. We were captivated.

We noticed at the far end of the little square a gleaming white building that seemed out of place. A sign on the building explained that this square was named in honor of Fado legend Maria Severa, who was born in this house in 1820 and lived in this neighborhood.

Her father was a gypsy, her mother owned a tavern and was a sex-worker known as *Barbuda*, "the bearded one." Maria, however, was a great beauty by all accounts, and perhaps unavoidably fell into her mother's profession. She sang early Fado songs in the taverns and brothels of the Mouraria. According to legend, she was the first person to sing Fado in the streets, accompanying herself on guitar and composing her own lyrics. She sang about her life and her problems: love and heartbreak, betrayal, jealousy, revenge, tragedy; the same problems as the people she lived among. Her style of Fado became wildly popular. Indeed, one has to wonder if strands of this acceptance of hardship that will break the soul might have gone all the way back to the moors left to fend for themselves on this ancient hill.

There are no portraits of Maria, but here are some vivid descriptions written by various writers who met her (with thanks to my source, the website www.atlaslisboa.com/severa-fado.):

When I entered Severa's house, a modest dwelling of the vulgar type her unlucky peers inhabit, there she was, smoking, leaning back on a straw couch, wearing polishing slippers dotted with red twine, a silk flowery kerchief on her head and the sleeves of her dress rolled up to the elbows. She was a rather swarthy, thin, nervous woman, remarkable for

her magnificent peninsular eyes. On the gaming table laid a guitar, the inseparable companion to her triumphs.
—Writer Luis Augusto Palmeirim

It will be difficult for another Severa to appear, haughty and impetuous, so generous as ready to punch the face of whoever would act rogue on her! Brave, full of affection for the ones she cared for, as well as rough to her enemies, She was no ordinary woman, you can be sure of that.
—Poet Bulhão Pato

One of her lovers was the Count of Vimioso, a "bohemian" aristocrat who used to take Maria out to watch bullfights. This gave her exposure to the world beyond the Mouraria. She was hired to sing at parties in high society, and her reputation grew. But tragically, Maria died of tuberculosis at the age of 26. According to legend, though, what she really died of was a broken heart, because the social difference between her and the count was never going to allow a marriage between them. In keeping with the soul of Fado, reputedly her final words were, "I die without ever having lived."

Something in her music quickened the heart of Lisbon. Fado changed because of her; it became this powerful expression of desire crushed by fate. Because of Maria, Fado moved from the shadows into popular culture. Her life became a legend, then the subject of a novel, then a play, which in 1933 was turned into the first Portugese movie ever made with sound.

As Teresa and I strolled from the little square that bore the legend's name, I thought about the shrines to these two Marias, just a few short blocks from one another. The people of Lisbon loved the Virgin Mary because she saved them from their fate. They loved Maria Severa because she *sang* to them about their fate. She transformed their sorrow into more than simply suffering. She made it into something beautiful, something holy.

Chapter 9

Sponge Taffy Cliffs of the Algarve

Massive slabs of sponge taffy: that was my first thought when I saw the glowing limestone cliffs that line the southwest coast of Portugal's Algarve. Like my favorite childhood treat, these yellow-red-tan cliffs are pocked through with holes. And crumbly, all too crumbly. Signs posted all along the seashore warn to keep your distance from the tops of the cliffs. More signs mark the bottoms, where great yellow chunks have fallen and lie strewn about the sand.

From 23 million to 5 million years ago, the whole area was submerged. Coral reefs built up, layer upon layer. Through millions of years they were crushed and hardened into slabs of limestone, hundreds of feet deep. Then as sea levels fell, the waves began pounding away at the shore, grinding stone into sand, and in the process creating some of the most dramatic beaches in the world.

All along the coast, where once there were only tiny fishing villages, tourist hotels and condos have sprung up by the tens of thousands in the past fifty years. First came the folks from Lisbon, building summer homes. Then came the Brits, Germans, Dutch, Danes, even the French, seduced not only by the beaches and warm sunny winters, but also by the lower cost of everything in Portugal compared to northern Europe. In recent decades Americans and Canadians have arrived. Whole flocks of "snowbirds," who prefer to fly across the Atlantic rather than spend their winters in the cold, roost here in the off-season, between November and March, when it's sunny and cool.

Collectively, these visitors have helped make tourism the biggest industry in Portugal. The cost, of course, has been

Algarve's cliffs and beaches

an almost endless building boom, much of it slapped up fast and cheap, with little apparent consideration for aesthetics. Concrete buildings now sit encrusted round almost every beach like mutant barnacles, stretching out in all directions.

Yet, the beaches remain beguilingly beautiful. The sheer instability of the cliffs necessitates that the condos and hotels stay back a safe distance from the edge, and are for the most part invisible from the shore. A few decades ago the national government also made the wise decision to preserve the natural parts of the coast where dunes and endangered pine forests now receive some protection (and make for fabulous hiking trails). As a result there are still large stretches where one can walk away from the crowds.

On our first day in the Algarve I learned to respect the edge, thanks to my babysitter. Ann McCullough last babysat me and my siblings in Toronto in 1969. But she also became a dear friend of my mother's, and so decades later Ann still keeps in touch with our family. She and her husband, George, are now Canadian Algarve snowbirds.

We met up for a cliff walk the morning after our arrival. Ann and George are in their seventies now, but I easily could have recognized them in a crowd. Ann is petite, under five feet tall, with boundless energy and zest for life. George is as wiry and lean as I remembered him fifty years ago. They pointed out two features of the cliffs I had not yet noticed. First, there were giant holes in the ground where the sea had carved out caverns from below, and then the tops had collapsed. Second, they showed me places where the cliff tops were undercut, as wind and water run-off eroded the exposed edge. In many places wooden fences have been erected around the danger zones, but many people just hop over them. My friends told me the tragic story of an American man they know who had walked too close and fell from the crumbling edge into the sea. His wife somehow scrambled down and pulled him from the water. He needed to be airlifted out, with broken bones and a head injury. It's a miracle that he survived.

I took their advice very much to heart. I've stood right on the edge of many a granite mountain viewpoint. But not on these cliffs! I realized that all these years later, Ann was still keeping me safe with a warning and a well-timed cautionary tale. Ann and George also told me that in some places tunnels through the limestone allow people to walk from beach to beach, and I found this to be so on the very first beach I visited. This tiny crevice opened up to the next beach with a spectacular arch on the other side (below).

Over the next ten days Teresa and I explored many beaches along the coast, including Sagres, the town where Prince Henry the Navigator built his famous school for navigators during Portugal's age of discovery. Beyond Sagres is Cabo de São Vicente, the furthest-west point in mainland Europe. The cliffs there are solid granite, and yet, by the lighthouse there is a small, somber plaque in memory of a young tourist who

The original golden arches

slipped and fell to his death on that spot. He was twenty-eight.

Our plan was to stay in several different towns along the coast, but we got waylaid when we arrived at our third destination, *Casa Três Palmeiras* (House of the Three Palms) in Portimão. This elegant B&B sits right on the clifftops. We were stunned by the view of the many sea stacks and the sculpted formations of the cliffs, some a virbrant rust red from iron deposits that have oxidized. And we were charmed by the hostess, Dolly Schlinensiepen, who was also the owner (below).

Dolly and her German husband built their home on this cliff in 1960. She tells me there was nothing here back then, and the beach below them became known as the "Beach of the German."

Dolly Schlinensiepen, owner and manager of Casa Três Palmeiras.

After her husband died, Dolly converted the house into a B&B. That was in 1985. She has been actively running the place ever since, including preparing our individual breakfasts, and having daily chats with the guests to make sure we are having a good time, offering advice as needed.

"Why don't you retire?" we asked her.

"Then what will I do?" she told us with a laugh. Her children like it that she keeps busy, and does not call them all the time, she joked. Then quietly she added, "and when I am here, I don't feel alone.... People come here as guests, and they leave as friends."

That was certainly true for Teresa and me.

Dolly said that at low tide you could walk from her beach around the cliffs and all the little coves, all the way to the far side of the main beach of Portimão, a good two-hour walk. And so one morning, as the tide was going out, I headed out to explore the caves and stacks along the shore.

Eventually, I reached the main Portimão beach and decided to turn back. Only at this point did I realize that the tide was not going out. All this time it was coming in! At outcroppings where there were no cave tunnels I had to slosh my way back around the cliffs, thigh deep in water. There was one crossing that was past my knees on the walk out. On the return, I realized it was waist deep. The ground was not sandy here, but rough with patches of limestone, so I had to feel my way slowly with bare feet. Occasional waves a few feet high crashed into the rock face beside me. I did not feel I was in actual danger, but I could have been banged up if the waves knocked me off my feet and threw me against the cliff.

At the deepest, most exposed point, I saw a big one coming. All I could do was brace both hands against the rock wall as the wave broke, and lean in. However, I had forgotten a fundamental lesson about *wave reflection* from my grade ten Physics class. The wave washed in to my shoulders, but then it washed *back* right in my face, full force. I staggered, feet churning for balance on the rocks, as I thrashed my way to the shore. I touched my sopping, bald head. My hat was gone. So were my sunglasses. But, other than a couple of cuts on my feet and a bruise on one leg, I was fine. More experienced, but not necessarily any the wiser. (Please, nobody tell Ann.)

Chapter 10

Silves Castle, Where the Past Is Present

Flâneur lesson #5: You can time travel

So much of flâneuring is learning to observe the world around you in the present moment. Yet the present has layers of the past embedded in it. The present is just the thinnest veneer of all that has gone before. If one only sees the glint of the veneer, one only catches a reflection of the surface and misses all that lies underneath. I felt this most acutely when Teresa and I visited the historic, quiet little town of Silves in the Algarve, located by the banks of the River Arade, just inland from the bustling beach towns of Portugal's southern coast.

The castle on the hilltop seems relatively modest compared to many of Portugal's grand fortresses. But it is actually one of the best preserved Moorish fortifications in the country. These red stone walls hold the excavated ruins of a once-thriving community that was the center of trade and culture on the edge of the Arabian world. In the eleventh century Silves was ruled by the poet Ibn Ammar, and the poems composed here were so sophisticated that Silves was considered the cradle of Arabian-Andalusian poetry. In the twelfth century, under the rule of Ibne Caci—poet, philosopher, and politician—the town was described as having rich palaces, mosques, fine houses, and beautiful women. *The Baghdad of the West*, it was called.

These ruins reveal traces of this past. It's easy to imagine cultured people going about their daily lives in these excavated streets, feeling safe inside the walls. Today, palm trees and gardens have been planted inside, giving the place an intimate atmosphere. There's even a modern sculpture garden and an outdoor café. In what is called the Palace of the Balconies, stands one lone white marble pillar. It supports a reconstructed arch with Moorish windows that emanates an aura of luxurious sophistication—at least for that brief, stable era of the castle's history.

A cistern in the middle of the castle grounds reveals that the citadel could withstand long seiges without running out of water. And indeed, Silves was besieged, again and again, as defenders fought attackers and the hilltop changed hands. A skeleton of a boy—probably a teenager—lying face down, with many broken bones, is on display at the nearby archeological museum. He was killed during one of these seiges. These walls ultimately provided only an illusion of security.

The museum tells the story of how Silves has been home to humans for many thousands of years. Long before Stonehenge, earily inhabitants erected giant stone menhirs decorated with swirling patterns on the Algarve landscape. Then followed the immigrating tribes of the Iron Age, probably Celts. The Phoenicians arrived from the Levant roughly 3,000 years ago, establishing ports along the coast in their quest for precious metals—copper and tin—with which they made bronze. Then the Greeks, Carthaginians, Romans and Visigoths each took over as their respective empires expanded and declined. The Moors replaced the Visigoths, ruling the region from Silves for some five hundred years. After much struggle they ultimately retreated before the advancing Portuguese, who together with Crusader knights from northern Europe "liberated" the land.

The Portuguese then promptly began their own seafaring quest for trade and precious metals, forging the world's first truly global empire. Prince Henry the Navigator, intrinsic to the success of this empire, governed the Algarve from Silves. Along the southwest castle wall are the foundations of what was supposedly Henry's house, including a spacious living room with the remains of a vaulted ceiling, and an olive oil press. As Portugal's empire in its turn declined, Silves lost its influence in the Algarve. For a while it flourished as a fishing town, then the center of the region's cork industry.

In recent decades the northern Europeans have returned as tourists, not crusaders—but still as saviors of Portugal's economy. Unfortunately, Silves can't compete with the beach towns on the coast. It's no longer the capital of the region, just a brief stop for tourists through the ruins of this once glorious citadel, and its three thousand years of history: a past that is still present.

Part II

Paris, France

Classic Flâneur

Chapter 11

A New Angel in Paris

Flâneur lesson #9: Walk without a destination

On arriving in Paris this week, I discovered the perfect book for me: *Flâneur: The Art of Wandering the Streets of Paris* by Federico Castigliano, an Italian who flânuered here for several years. Reading Chapter 1, I realized I have so much to learn. *Mature Flâneur?* Ha! *Rank Amateur Flâneur* is more like it! Here, from Chapter 1:

> I thought the destiny of every true flâneur was to immerse himself in the panorama surrounding him, to the point of becoming one with it and, ultimately, to vanish. To listen to the voice of the world, the self must be silenced. And the flâneur is the incarnation of this ideal: dazzled by beauty, he decides to relinquish the self... Lost in the maze of the city, he progressively sheds all the teaching received and adheres to the visible reality as a chameleon. The man who wanders the city projects himself on the façades of the building, on the shop windows sparkling in their sequence, on the faces of the people who pass by. It is precisely this ability to annul oneself, to come out of the stifling prison of the inner life, this is the science and skill of the flâneur.

Holy crap. A flâneur is a Zen monk!

In Chapter 2, Castigliano sets forth what is required: "First of all, move randomly":

The flâneur moves through the city with neither a map nor a plan. He has to feel himself to be free and alone, ready and willing for the imponderable... There exists a mysterious energy in chance, a secret correspondence that connects the elements of the outside world with the inner being of the walking man. It is therefore indispensable to push oneself toward ever new realities, to do that which the ordinary person would not do.

He says, bluntly, that "flâneurie is not to be confused with tourism":

Most people are completely incapable of walking without a destination and exploring the underside of a city. It is difficult to find a true flâneur, i.e., a person capable of freeing himself from the chain of material requirements and needs to the point of acquiring a vision of the world that is not strictly functional. Only a flâneur is able to establish an intimate relationship with the city that leads him to adapt his own mood, his own interior being to that of the place. The city belongs to the flâneur, but the flâneur becomes, in his turn, part of the city...

Breathless, I closed my iPad. Time to give it a whirl... but not a *purposeful* whirl.

It was raining lightly, gray and cold. Near the Bastille monument, where our apartment is, there's an old raised tramline that has been converted into a miles-long, linear garden walk. I used to run along this line, in the days before my inevitable torn meniscus. I'd jog out to the end of the line and back, just like a tram on a track. Most of the time, my mind would drift as I ran: courses to teach, books to write, my to-do list. Oh, sure, I enjoyed the flowers, the architecture, the rare sunset. But basically, I was a busy man in motion. Today, I set off down the line at a slower pace.

When I got to a park about a mile down the path, I found the gate on the path that I usually take was locked. Normally, if this gate is locked, I retrace my steps and take an alternate route I know. This time, I did something I never did before. I followed a path to the right instead, which led me to a part of the park I never knew existed. It overlooked a street below, and on that street, I saw a new angel.

I say a *new* angel because Paris must have a thousand statues of angels, and not just in churches and museums. You find them in sculpture gardens and cemeteries, on bridges and fountains, and, of course, perched all over the buildings. There are literally

Angel in the square of the 12th Arrondissment City Hall.

angels in the architecture. It's not a metaphor in Paris, Paul Simon! For awhile, Teresa and I started collecting photos of Paris angels, and Teresa turned some of hers into art photographs. We have them hanging on our walls. So, I spot angels in Paris better than most other things. But in perhaps fifty runs through this park over the years, I'd never set eyes on this one before.

She stood just above the street corner, facing traffic next to a small playground surrounded by a few trees; a slide, a sandbox, nothing fancy. Life-sized, her bronze surface now green with age, the angel wore a golden laurel wreath on her head. She held up a second wreath—a symbol of victory—in both hands, as if offering it to heaven.

What was she doing here, on this nondescript city street? Why wasn't she spreading her wings above the lintel of some cathedral doorway?

The description on her modest marble pedestal, roughly translated, reads: "To the children of the 12th *Arrondissement"* — the number for this district of Paris—"who died for France, 1914–1918 and 1939–1945." The memorial was somber and beautiful, but I wondered, why place it next to a playground?

I walked around the park to a large brick building at the front, French flags flapping from the roof in the rain. Ah, the *Mairie* of the 12th! The district municipal headquarters. This makes it a suitable location for a memorial. I turned back to face the little playground, and noticed near the entrance a white plaque. It contained a long list of names.

With even my rudimentary French, I could tell this was another memorial. It was for the 350 children of the district who had been arrested and deported by Vichy government police during the Nazi occupation in 1942–1944. In all of France, over 11,000 children, mostly Jewish, were taken from their homes and killed in the death camps during those years. Sixty of the children taken from this district were pre-schoolers. Their names and ages were written on this plaque. *Ne Les Oublion Jamais*, it reads. "Never forget them."

I imagined this park on a sunny day, filled with young children laughing and playing while their parents watch, and the ghosts of the children who never returned.

The wind picked up. The rain fell harder. People huddled glumly under the thin dry strips of concrete next to buildings as I walked in a bee-line back to our cosy apartment. No more random wandering for me today. By the time I was home, the cold and wet had penetrated my shoes. Perhaps a little more of Paris had penetrated me, too.

Chapter 12

Josephine Baker Takes Her Place in the Pantheon

Teresa and I made a pilgrimage to the Pantheon to pay tribute to the American singer, dancer, and decorated war-hero, the barrier-busting Josephine Baker. On Tuesday November 30, 2021, the American singer became the sixth woman to enter the Pantheon, which houses the remains of over 1,500 writers, scientists, and artists, honored for their contributions to the world. Baker shattered racial barriers as a jazz icon in 1920s Paris, joined in the struggle against the Nazis in the 1940s, and marched with Martin Luther King during the anti-racist struggles of the 1960s. She was the only woman to speak at the famous March on Washington organized by King in 1963. There, she said:

> You know, friends, that I do not lie to you when I tell you I have walked into the palaces of kings and queens and into the houses of presidents. And much more. But I could not walk into a hotel in America and get a cup of coffee, and that made me mad. And when I get mad, you know that I open my big mouth.

"She made the right choices at every turn of history, always distinguishing light from darkness," declared French President Emmanuel Macron at the ceremony honoring Baker, who died in 1975. She was, he said, an "incarnation of the 'French spirit.'" Why did it take 46 years after her death for France to recognize Baker's accomplishments? I guess it's harder for nations to distinguish light from darkness than it is for heroic individuals.

The Pantheon is one of the most striking landmarks in Paris: a giant dome on a hilltop south of the Seine, visible from much of the city. Originally the building was commissioned as a cathedral to the patron saint of Paris, St. Genevieve. In 451 A.D. she spurred the besieged citizens on to mass prayer gatherings that prevented the Huns from sacking the city. Genevieve also acted as a go-between and negotiator between the king and the invaders, preserving Paris from those who would have destroyed it. She clearly possessed a remarkable combination of saintly and secular talents.

Like so many of Paris' iconic structures, control of the Pantheon bounced back and forth between spiritual and civic authorities in the turbulent eighteenth and nineteenth centuries until ultimately it was repurposed as a secular temple to honor Paris' great men and, eventually, its great women… though so far only six women have been granted space in what was once St. Genevieve's place, including Ms. Baker. It seems to me there is still a lot of catching up to do!

Gorgeous mosaics cover the interior walls of the Pantheon with scenes of the deeds of St. Genevieve and Clovis I, the king she aided. It was he who united the Gauls into a single French kingdom that eventually became France. The interior sculptures, however, were added later. Instead of religious figures, the stonework honors the likes of Rousseau and Diderot. Massive stone tableaus pay tribute to the Revolution and the establishment of the modern French republic based on *liberté, égalité, fraternité* (note to Macron: Is there a French term for *siblinghood* we could replace *fraternité* with *s.v.p.*?).

Just as moving, to me, is the place of honor given to science. At the center of the Pantheon, a pendulum swings, its top end attached to the domed ceiling, 67 meters up. This is a replica of Foucault's Pendulum. Indeed, the Pantheon is where the great French physicist made his original demonstration that proved the earth spins in an orbit. The math is quite complicated, but the idea is simple: as the giant pendulum swings, it does not move perfectly back and forth. Instead it veers a little to one side with every oscillation, gradually ticking round like the minute hand on a clock. Why? Because the earth itself is turning slowly. The swing of the pendulum on a long thread captures this motion which would be inexplicable if it happened on a stationary earth. For the experiment to work, it required a very long pendulum, and absolutely no wind interference. *Voila*, the Pantheon was perfect for the task.

We found the stairs at the rear of the Pantheon that spiral down to the crypt where the bodies of the saints of science, arts and politics are interred. This is not some dank bone chamber. The walls are the same creamy-smooth limestone as the church above. The light is pleasant, neither dim nor glaring. The atmosphere is rather like what one would encounter at an efficient corporate headquarters, everything immaculate and professional. We were greeted first by Voltaire and Rousseau, at either side of the entrance. From there, some 1,500 underground tombs stretched out before us in orderly rows. There were people milling about, all wearing masks, but it was not too crowded.

Eventually we wound our way towards Josephine Baker's niche, which is empty, of course, except for the plaque (she was buried in Monaco in 1975, and the French would not have been so rude to have dug her up and moved her). We found an extravagant wreath, laid by her niche courtesy of the mayor of San Francisco. What made the wreath unusual was a cluster of gold bananas hanging from the center. Baker was famous in Paris for her song-and-dance in a skimpy "banana skirt." Right. The wild African savage in the salons of Paris. It seems so horrific to our sensibilities. How did she endure it? As one French tribute to Baker explained, she danced in the banana skirt "ironically." The French recognized that, and loved her for it.

And why the wreath from the mayor of San Francisco? Baker, who was also bisexual, was honored in the city's Rainbow Honor Walk with a large bronze plaque in 2019. She was a barrier buster indeed. She's an American in Paris, well honored. A woman who deserved her place in the Pantheon.

Josephine Baker at the Pantheon: a real American in Paris.

Chapter 13

An Accidental Art Walk in Paris

Flâneur lesson # 7 Find art everywhere

Today, my second day after a positive Covid diagnosis, I took a walk along the disused train line near our Paris apartment that has been converted into the *Coulée Verte* (Green Belt). It's a three-mile-long linear park lined with trees and foliage that sits atop an old viaduct. I feel lucky, because the self-quarantine regulations for Covid cases allow a max of two hours a day outside for exercise. Obviously, I pick a time of day when it's not crowded, and I don't get close to anyone.

I used to jog along this route on previous visits to Paris, before my inevitable torn meniscus forced me to give up running. Walking helps me appreciate the journey more, which is what flâneuring is all about. The last time I struck out this way, I found an unexpected angel. So who knows what will happen next if I just follow my nose?

Indeed, half an hour into my walk, I noticed a lovely stone building with fresh blue trim on the windows on the other side of a little playground. I scooted down Rue Brahms to the front of it and discovered it was an old, small train station that had been repurposed as a community center. I took a picture, and then, on my walk back toward the park, I noticed a stunning set of art photographs displayed on the iron bars at the front of the station.

They were a series of still-life photos (*nature morte* in French, which sounds to me like "dead nature"). But, replacing the traditional flower vase in such scenes, each of these photos featured a plastic bottle. The sign on the exhibit, by photographer

Ludovic Alussi, explained: "Plastic has become an integral part of our life, our bodies, our environment." Though beautiful to behold, the bottles "symbolize our comfortable indifference and ease in the face of the problem of our overconsumption."

What made the photos so discomfiting is how nature and plastic combine in these works with such stunning beauty. It's jarring. I think of all the plastic pollution campaigns I've seen, all my memories of plastic trash. I guess that's the point.

Art on a fence.

Art under a bridge.

I loved the idea that these provocative, stunning works of art were just slung on an iron fence. The photos were printed on metal, so impervious to the elements, and screwed securely into the fence at the back. But still, this was just a nondescript little street on the edge of town, and suddenly, *voila!*, some world-class art and social critique for all passersby to ponder.

Thoughtfully, I trudged back to the path, where it widens into more of a park. A park sign read: "Observe life in the protected spaces." Well, this was surely a sign for me, too. Look around! Suddenly, and I mean suddenly, I noticed there was art everywhere. I'm not speaking metaphorically. And I don't mean spray paint graffitti. I mean interesting, playful, beautiful, art. Honestly, I felt as if I suddenly woke up. The trail went under a bridge at this point, where I found over a dozen paintings like this one, above, on the tunnel walls.

As I turned around and began my walk back to my Covid confinement, the sun came out—pretty rare for Paris in December. The intense light further illuminated the path, and I saw for the first time art that I had honest-to-God walked right past, blindly, on my outbound journey. These whimsical masterpieces could just as well have been hanging in any gallery in Paris.

This accidental art walk totally reoriented my bouts of flâneuring through Paris. Normally, my attention was focused on the palaces, cathedrals, museums, and grand hotels on the boulevards. But now, I turned my attention to the gritty side streets. To many, Paris' backways are ugly. Not to me, not any more. They too contain works of art, but you have to look out for them. Much of it is unofficial—guerrilla art, you could call it. It wears off quickly, and the distressed, worn edges become part of the overall effect. I'd like to be clear that this street art is different from graffiti. Yes, there are plenty of desperate signatures scrawled on the walls. But I'm referring to genuine works of art: dramatic, playful, subversive, and sometimes surprisingly, sweet.

Flânuering has helped me slow down enough that I can find these hidden gems. In street art, I read the hearts of many creative souls who have made the city their canvas and their home. They tell their stories, express their dreams, and play their subtle jokes for those with eyes to see.

Art everywhere in the streets of Paris.

Chapter 14

Cracks That Let in the Light

Flâneur lesson #8: Pursue the unexpected

The first day I finally tested negative for Covid I felt mighty fine. Truth be told, though I remained asymptomatic, I felt kind of like a pariah during my ten days of isolation, unable to enter stores, restaurants, even taxis. With Omicron now in my rear view mirror, I set out on an ambitious walk following the canal route north from the Bastille monument up Richard Lenoir Blvd. A few kilometers in, a crack in the sidewalk stopped me dead in my tracks. The dull gray path next to the drab gray road under the dreary gray sky contained a shiny patch of light.

I felt suddenly alert, as if I had just spotted some elusive bird flitting about under forest cover. How easily I could have missed this! I could have been lost in thought, checking text messages while I walked, looking at my map app, or simply distracted by the seagulls on the canal. I crept up on the crack, as if not to send it fluttering out of sight. This is it:

The crack

Bending down, I could see how the tiny, white, tan and red tiles had been expertly inlaid in a complex pattern, perfectly filling the crack. Notice how the edges of tiles have been individually cut to fit snugly inside the border? Somebody found this gritty, damaged little space and patched it up with craftsmanship and beauty. What a gift, for whoever stops to notice.

This crack woke me up. What might Paris reveal to me today, if I kept my eyes open? A little further along the road, I noticed a larger-than-life bronze statue half hidden behind some rosebushes. It was in the midst of a wide open square, surrounded by ordinary apartment buildings. Now, Paris is full of statues in little parks and squares everywhere. Mostly, I vaguely notice them, and just walk past. But the little crack inspired me to go over and take a closer look. Who was this bald, round-faced guy on a pedestal?

The plaque read: *Raoul Follereau, L'Apotre des Lepreux.* "The Apostle of Leprosy." Well, now I'm glad I carry my phone with me after all, because Wikipedia explained that in the 1940s, Follereau, a devout Catholic, founded an organization that took care of lepers around the world. But he was not a doctor nor a missionary. He was an author, a writer of plays and poetry, and founder of various literary and cultural societies across Latin America. Sometime in the 1930s, on a trip through the region, Follereau's car broke down. From out of the forest, a small group of disfigured people emerged:

> To the guide I [Follereau] said: "Who are these men?" — "Lepers" he replied... "But wouldn't they be better in the village? What have they done to be excluded?" — "They are lepers," answered the taciturn and stubborn man... and it was on that day that I decided to plead only one cause, one cause for all my life, that... of lepers.
> —Étienne Thévenin, *Éditions Fayard*

The encounter changed his life. Follereau worked for decades to raise funds to create villages for the victims of leprosy, long shunned and cast out from their home communities. He lectured tirelessly at conferences around the globe, seeking to remove the stigma and fear the disease aroused. He launched World Leprosy Day in 1953, a day dedicated to prayer for the afflicted, and to mobilize efforts for treatment, since a cure was discovered in 1952. Yes, a cure—but how do you get that cure to those in the remote corners of the world where the disease persists?*

Follereau, the writer, used his pen to advance his cause. He wrote public letters to US President Eisenhower and USSR

---

* Though the prevalence of leprosy has diminished 90% in the past thirty years, some seven million people still suffer from the now-curable disease, mostly in poor, tropical nations. There are approximately 200,000 new cases each year, and the social stigma of the disease remains a major obstacle to its eradication.

President Khrushchev, asking them to each donate the cost of one "bombing plane." With this money, he implored, "we could treat all the lepers in the world." He never got a response, but these letters—and others he wrote to world leaders—fueled public support for his cause. His clever tactic of comparing funding for military hardware with the cost of humanitarian goals also became widely adopted by other charities.

Over forty years in all, Follereau's foundations raised over three billion euros to treat leprosy. In 1997, to mark the twentieth anniversary of Follereau's death, former Beninese President Mathieu Kérékou said: "The legacy he left us... is the battle against leprosy and the promotion of a world of love, solidarity and tolerance."

Follereau found a crack in the pavement, and filled it with light.

Chapter 15

Paris Twilight Zone

Flâneur lesson #11: Yield to the whim

Twilight is the best time to be a flâneur in Paris. It's a time of transition, the gap between what Parisians did today, and what they will be doing this evening. Normally in winter it's cold, windy, rainy. Nobody lingers. They hunch and hurry. But today it has been near sixty degrees and sunny. So the approaching night draws people out, including a flâneur. I am discovering that as I practice the fine art of wandering aimlessly through a city, just observing, sometimes I begin to disappear, and in a sense become a part of the city itself.

I started out with a plan to head south across the Seine to the Jardin des Plantes, with its large botanical gardens. But 100 meters out the door, just past the Bastille monument, I swung west instead. I remembered there was a pile of stones I wanted to see down Blvd. Henry IV. I'm learning, you see, that it is absolutely fine for a flâneur to head out the door with a plan. Just don't plan on sticking with the plan. One must *yield to the whim*.

There's a tiny park at the bridge where Blvd. Henry IV meets the river. It's called Square Henry-Galli. It is a postage stamp of a green patch, barely worthy of the designation "square." I've walked past it hundreds of times, because it's the direct path to Notre Dame and all the hot spots of the Left Bank. Never once have I noticed the pile of cut stones at the edge of the park, nor the small plaque, unreadable from the street, announcing that these are foundation stones from the Bastille fortress, discovered in 1899 during construction nearby.

The Bastille fortress, of course, was the famous armory and prison that the people of Paris stormed, the event which precipitated the 1789 French Revolution. This is why Bastille Day, July 14, is France's Independence Day. The Bastille metro station contains a long mural, portraying the events of the Revolution, including the storming of the Bastille. But the massive fortress itself, you won't find that anywhere. Why?

So hated was this symbol of the king's power that after the Revolution the entire Bastille fortress was torn down by the citizens of Paris and obliterated. Every stone was removed, including the foundations. They were spread across the city, used for bridges, streets and buildings, so that nothing remained. This little pile of foundation stones in front of me is one of the very few vestiges you can identify today that mark this event that started the Revolution.

I walked along the Right Bank, not sure how far I might travel towards central Paris, until I was captivated by the lights on Rue du Pont Louis-Phillippe. Then, turning towards the Seine, I saw across the bridge, on the Left Bank, the glorious Pantheon dome in the distance, undergirded by the dancing holiday streetlights. And there on the bridge, in the middle of it all, I spied a real-life Emily in Paris, her béret-covered head down, pondering how she will respond to a text, as if her phone filled up the entire world.

Crossing the Pont Louis-Philippe, I could see people strolling along the Seine. One of the wonderful things Mayor Hidalgo has done for Paris is close off many roads to cars, including the expressway that runs along the Right Bank. She's also replaced many traffic lanes with bicycle lanes throughout the city, incurring the ire of many drivers, who fume as they sit in traffic jams while the bikers whizz by. Hidalgo's ultimate goal is to make Paris a car-free, green city. *Bonne chance*, Madame Mayor!

The bridge leads to the western tip of Ile Saint-Louis, one of two small islands in the heart of Paris. I stroll along to the eastern tip, and then cross the bridge towards the Left Bank, where there is a spectacular view of Notre Dame in the midst of her makeover since the disastrous fire of 2019. I am moving back towards the Bastille now, but on the opposite bank of the river.

There's an open-air sculpture garden along this stretch, with wide, pleasant walkways. Here and there, young couples sit close, swinging their legs over the water. I hear drumming, and in a little square just up the bank I come across a dozen or so Africans hanging out and making music, invoking the rhythms of home. Back by the water's edge, I see that one of the dockside little amphitheaters is being used for a tango dance class. Couples glide smoothly over the concrete under the park lights, though one wrong backwards twirl might put them into the drink!

I cross the Austerlitz Bridge back to the Right Bank at the Jardin des Plantes, my original destination—without even bothering to go in—and head back towards the Bastille monument. The route passes over a Metro grating that wafts warm air up from the train lines below. On top of the grating, homeless people have erected several small domed camping tents. It's a grim reality: hundreds of homeless men and women spend the winter on the streets. But a least the Metro exhaust keeps them warm.

Taking the pathway down to the canal that runs toward the Bastille, I find couples and families out for a quiet evening stroll before dinner. Lights twinkle on the boats in their moorings. A small group of twentysomethings sits on the steps, drinking beer. A couple dances to a boombox, the music not so loud as to be obnoxious. A few joggers stretch on the stairways, then prance along in that unique way the French have of running, like show horses. On a quiet corner I spot a woman with her dog, listening to music on her headphones. She seems utterly content in her solitude, gazing out at a decorated Christmas tree on one of the boats.

Back on the Place de la Bastille, I see that it is being stormed by... skateboarders! Perhaps two dozen kids in their teens and twenties skate round and round, practicing their jumps and aerial manoeuvres on the concrete pylons that are placed there exactly for that purpose. I'm happy to see several young women among them, skating with their male peers.

On the far side of the monument, I pass the Bastille Opera. Despite the pandemic, there is a huge crowd lined up for the evening performance. They chatter expectantly. Beyond that, I enter my own neighborhood, its streets lined with bars, restaurants, and dance clubs that make this district so popular with young Parisans, who have as little fear of the pandemic as the opera-goers. Covid be damned, the French cannot sacrifice the essentials of civilization!

I pause for a moment to feel the thrum of conversation that surrounds me. It feels physical, the vibations of a thousand voices speaking all at once, each wrapped in its own intense conversation and yet together making the sound of Paris, a composition as distinct as a symphony.

It is fully dark as I reach the iron gates of the little cour where we have our apartment. I've been immersed in the city more than two hours. Stepping onto the cobblestones of this little street, with its cheery holiday lights transports me back home: to Teresa, dinner, a bottle of wine, and to myself.

Chapter 16

Medieval Fair Frolic in Provins

I've been to a lot of "Renaissance" festivals in the US, where young people wear their fantasy wardrobes—cloaks and kilts, bustiers and broadswords. You eat a turkey drumstick with your hands and wash it down with mead or ale, maybe buy some Celtic jewelry. Makeshift castles and Tudor-beamed buildings are thrown up to give it a fantasy-medieval atmosphere, and it's all good fun.

Alors! Those fairs have *nothing* on the town of Provins, a *real* medieval village in the suburbs of Paris, with a *real* medieval market that started in the twelfth century. This past weekend was their spring fair, and we were not going to miss it. Teresa and I went with two friends from Paris, Kerstin and Zerina.

It's an easy 90-minute train ride from the city, and on this warm spring day, we made it a point to get there early to beat the maurading hordes. However, since this was still March, there were relatively few tourists anyway, at least compared to the summer festival, which is typically packed, at least in non-plague years.

The best medieval features of Provins are the massive fortress-keep called the Cesar Tower, the giant Saint-Ayoul Priory, and the impressive stone ramparts that still surround much of the village. So much of the town has been preserved that the whole area has been declared a UNESCO World Heritage Site. How did this happen, when Paris itself has preserved very little of its medieval history?

It turns out *bad economic policy* preserved Provins. The village stood at a trading crossroads in Roman times, and by the Medieval era, under the protection of the Counts of

Champagne, Provins began to host agricultural and goods fairs three times a year. The fairs grew to become crucial to the whole region's economy. Because of all this trade Provins also became a banking center, minting its own coins. The "denier provinois," was widely accepted throughout Europe. The fairs flourished from 1120 until 1320, when King Philip IV imposed harsh taxes that literally decimated Provins. Most residents packed up and left, and the town shrank from about 130,000 to 13,000 residents—the size it is today. Wars and political instability prevented the town from ever recovering. As a result, its ancient buildings were never demolished to make way for new ones. Several hundred years later, this relic of the past has awakened, surprisingly intact.

For my companions, the best thing about this historic town was... *the beams*! I forgot to mention, Kerstin and Zerina are both real estate agents, and Teresa is basically a wannabe agent. She scrolls through Paris apartment sites daily, and we can never just walk past an agent's office without looking at the photos of places for sale in the windows. Old buildings are at a premium in Paris, and there are suprisingly few with exposed wooden beams on the exterior. Most have been destroyed by fires or demolished in construction booms. But in Provins, whole streets are lined with them. For Teresa and Zerina, it was as if they had arrived in the real-estate version of the Emerald City, Eldorado, Disney World! They "oooh-ed" and "aaah-ed" at each old wooden house we passed like excited children.

"You two Americans," said Kerstin, who owns her own agency in Paris, "you go crazy over old houses!" She rolled her eyes.

"But, we don't have *any* buildings this old in the entire US!" Zerina replied, her enthusiasm undimmed.

Soon we reached the heart of the medieval market, which revolves around the town square, with its exquisitely restored

Provins festival: beams everywhere.

ancient buildings, now converted into restaurants and artisan shops. There were *beams, beams everywhere!*

In ages past, the market action in Provins took place underground. Merchants rented out the stone cellars beneath the townspeople's homes to store their perishable goods until market day, as these large subterranean spaces were natural coolers. For the present-day markets, these spaces are converted into artisan arcades. Merchant stalls offered everything from traditional embroidery, leatherwork and swords, to books, CDs, and T-shirts embossed with Celtic runes: about a thousand years' worth of variety.

A small, grassy park just off the main square had been converted into a medieval village, with blacksmiths and glass blowers, armor makers, and a couple of cooks who were roasting and selling strips of steak over an open fire like some eleventh-century McDonalds.

Good wi-fi in the medieval market.

This was a great place to find the hard-core participants of the festival in their full gear. They dressed variously as monks and knights, serving wenches and ladies in their finery—but also as bagpipe-playing Celts, Wiccans and, weirdly, a group of Mongolian musicians dressed as if from the court of Genghis Khan.

What I enjoyed most was the commitment and sense of fun of those who come to fairs like this in order to embody a past that they feel strongly connected to. Bustiers and leather armor suit them so much better than jeans and T-shirts. It's a wonderful thing that they can come to a genuine medieval town like Provins, hang out, play the pipes or engage in a little light swordplay, and feel at home—even if they must bring their smartphones with them.

Chapter 17

Why Are There Naked People on the Walls?

The naked woman and the toddler hanging off the fifth storey looked down at me. Directly beneath her was another woman, equally naked. Below her, was what appeared to be a duck, its wings frozen in stone, mid-flap. I gawked back up at them and laughed. This building façade was not some fancy palace or cathedral where you might expect angels, saints or gargoyles peering from the balustrades. This was an ordinary apartment

Naked people on Rue Perrée.

in the Haute Marais, a residential part of the city. Only in Paris, I thought, would you see such extravagant artistry on such an ordinary building (above).

You know how it is when you buy a new car, and suddenly you notice all the other cars of the same model on the road? Well, I started spotting naked people hanging off the walls of Paris' most mundane buildings: residences, offices, and in one case, a police station. Here's two examples from different parts of the city:

In the 10th Arrondissement (above left), there's no info, not even a plaque, that marks #48 Rue des Petites Ecuries. But I noticed that these are the Roman divinities Ceres (food) and Hermes (medicine). So maybe this was some kind of a dry goods company office? Note the needles on their upraised elbows. These prevent pigeons from landing on the statues and pooping on them.

Left, #48 Rue des Petites Ecuries; Right, clock on Rue d'Universite.

In the 7th Arrondissement, on Rue d'Universite, this was the office of a business-directory compiler! Look at the sculptures blowing a trumpet and scattering copies around the clock. They sure seem to be making a fuss about their publication!

What many of these buildings had in common was their date of construction: between 1890–1910. This was when *Art Nouveau* was all the rage in Paris. Indeed, naturalistic and extravagant façades were part of that movement. I vaguely remembered one famous *Art Nouveau* façade that appears in all the Paris guidebooks, on 29 Avenue Rapp, near the Eiffel Tower, so I ankled round to take a look.

The extravagant façade of 29 Avenue Rapp.

How deliciously extravagant for the home of a middle-class ceramics-maker, I thought. At least this building had a plaque. It stated that this residence won the Paris prize for best façade in 1903. A little online research revealed that this contest began in 1898, shortly after the authoritarian rules governing Paris' architectural style had been relaxed.

Wait—there were *laws* governing architectural style in Paris? *Absolutement.* In the mid-to-late 1800s, Baron Georges-Eugène Haussmann was empowered by Napoleon III to tear down the remnants of medieval Paris' wooden houses and construct a new city of broad boulevards and endless blocks of monolithic buildings. He built *eighty kilometers* of new streets in all, containing 40,000 homes, comprising 60% of the housing in Paris today. It was *forbidden* to insert statues or other architectural flourishes on these new buildings.

The city's architects rankled under these draconian rules that stifled their creativity. Indeed, Haussmann became extremely unpopular in Paris, both for turning the city into a construction zone for twenty years and for spending billions of francs. In the end, he was removed from office and the architects ran wild! For them, a new era of freedom and exuberance had begun.

In sum, these human faces on the façades are the faces of rebellion, and the flourishing of a new-found freedom for architecture at the dawn of twentieth-century Paris.

There is one other building I had seen many times, and long wondered about. This police station in the 12th Arrondissement has a row of identical, massive statues lining the top floor (below).

Why did that row of statues seem so familiar, I wondered? Riding the Metro one day, I found the answer. I was gazing out the window as we passed through the Louvre-Rivoli station and I saw a copy of the exact same statue from the station wall! It was part of a display featuring treasures of the museum. After

Police station in the 12th Arrondissement.

a quick search online, I discovered it was an exact replica of Michelangelo's *Dying Slave*—considered one of the Italian master's greatest sculptures, and one of the most important treasures of the Louvre.

I discovered that the police station was designed in 1985 by the post-modern architects Manuel Nuñez Yanowski and Miriam Teitelbaum. They proposed the outragrous idea of adding multiples of Michelangelo's famous statue to the otherwise bland building. The plan was resisted at first. I gather that the concern was that these top floors were to be the residences of police officers. Would they want to look out their windows and come eye to eye with nude male torsos every day? President Mitterrand himself weighed in—in favor of the project—but the statues were ultimately added to the façade in such a way that no male genitalia would be dangling from the rooftop. "So as not to shock the politicians," Yanowski has been quoted as saying.

But, just a minute! For the past 120 years no one in Paris seems the least bit shocked by all the naked women with their breasts hanging out from the walls of so many buildings. This is quite a double standard, Paris!

Alors, what have I learned from all this craning of the neck? Indeed, Paris is a rare city because its architecture is also art. And this is not only true for the monuments. The city has been built with extraordinary flourishes in the most ordinary of places. And behind each of these façades there lies a story ready to be discovered by any flâneur who looks up and wonders why.

Chapter 18

Stress and the Mature Flâneur

Flâneur lesson #12: Do one thing at a time

Teresa woke one fine spring day in Paris with an eye infection so nasty and inflamed we decided to go to a hospital emergency room. Figuring out how to do that in Paris was not at all easy. It was going to be our first use of our travel medical insurance, so I had to confirm what we needed to have with us, locate insurance cards and so on. Luckily, Norma, a dear friend on our *cour*, helped us find the best private eye hospital in the city for English speakers. I'm making it sound rather straightforward, but going through it all was a wrench: first because Teresa was complaining, and she *never, ever complains* about physical pain. You could cut off her arm, and she would just take some Advil and suck it up. So that had me worried.

Also, we were in the midst of packing and cleaning the apartment for a month-long trip to Italy, just two days away. I had to make plans, I had things to organize, last minute car rental details to confirm. I was discombobulated, and I was anxious about my beloved. Was she going to be okay? Would I have to cancel train tickets? Would our insurance card work? My anxiety was building into an overwhelming ball.

"Just focus now on getting Teresa to the hospital. Do only this one thing," said a voice in my head.

It created such clarity. Everything else dropped away. The present moment became uncluttered. In this clearing, I could find Teresa without all these other worries crowding my head, and just be with her in her distress while we headed for the taxi stand.

We did that one thing; we found the emergency admission desk at the eye hostpital. Teresa took a number. Due to Covid restrictions, I had to wait outside on the terrace. She joined me about 20 minutes later. Untreated. She said the receptionist told her it would cost 2,000 euros to see a doctor, and the wait time would be about six hours. Pay first, *bien sur*. She then gave Teresa the address of a public emergency eye clinic that would be much cheaper. Welcome to the French health care system! Our motto: *We don't really care about your money; we just don't want you to bother us.*

So Teresa left. She told me her eye was starting to feel better, anyway. Indeed, I could see the swelling had somewhat reduced in the past few hours, so we decided to take a stroll for the rest of the morning and just relax. Fortunately, the hospital was right across the road from one of our favorite parks that we had been meaning to visit all spring. And so, we moved on to the next one thing—take a walk in the park. And then the next....

Yes, this was a lucky outcome (Teresa's eye has recovered, slowly). For me, that piece of advice I gave to myself has stuck. Not just in emergencies or under stress, but also while flâneuring. I just do the one thing I'm doing. I don't get distracted by whatever looms on the horizon next in the day. If I'm out for a walk, I don't check my phone for emails. I just do one thing at a time. That helps me stay present, and only while I'm in the present, can I truly enjoy the moment. After all, we call it the *present*: because it's a gift.

I used to feel like a master of multitasking, juggling a dozen things with alacrity. I didn't feel stressed, but was it perhaps taking a toll on me nonetheless? Maybe adrenaline was overriding and masking my anxiety? I do recall times when I was working my hardest, I would suddenly break out in itchy hives all over my legs and belly. Hmmm.

I remember a Zen parable I heard years ago that makes the same point: It is the story of a monk whose job was to make breakfast for his monastery. One morning, while stirring the rice pot, a Boddhisattva appeared to him, hovering over the stove. The astonished monk paused for a second, then took his ladel and beat the divinity until He disappeared. Then the monk resumed stirring the rice. Moral: no matter what, don't be distracted from the task at hand.

For this mature flâneur, the path ahead is quite clear. Do. One. Thing. At. A. Time.

Chapter 19

Happy Couple Statues in Paris

I have been on a sculpture jag recently, looking at Paris' public statues. Mostly this is because the pandemic has made me shy of museums, but also because the weather is lovely in April, and so as I flâneur through the city, I regularly stumble upon amazing works of sculpture on public display. And while it is not polite to stare at people, let alone walk right up to them and take their picture, this behavior is perfectly fine with statues.

What I find most fascinating in statues of couples is the way the space between them expresses so much about their relationship. How they orient their arms, torsos, legs, the tilt

The Two Trees, or *Les Deux Arbres*, **symbolizes love and unity.**

of their heads: it all conveys a sense of movement, intention, feeling. In this way, a well-made statue can sometimes seem more real than actual human beings, just like a beautiful "still life" vase of sunflowers by Van Gogh seems more breathtaking that actual flowers in a pot.

I'd like to share with you some of my favorites found throughout the city.

The Two Trees (above): This sweet and simple couple can be found kissing on an island in the *Bois de Boulogne*. Situated between two trees at the water's edge, it would be easy to miss them altogether as you stroll along the shore. Boaters like to paddle close for a better look at the couple. The bronze pair, created by Gudmar Olovson, are tall and willowy, and barely brush together as they kiss. Even from across the water you can see how tenderly they hold each other, his hands on her shoulders, hers on his waist.

***

Next, I discovered a magnificent cluster of four couple statues on the strip of park, *Esplanade Gaston Monnerville*, that runs south from the *Jardin du Luxembourg*. Because the park is just a little bit out of the way from the main garden, I'd never actually walked through it before this April. I was totally captivated by the glowing white, larger-than-life marble couples against the backdrop of new green leaves. Each statue is named for a time of day—Dawn, Day, Twilight, and Night—and depicts, rather playfully, relations between a man and a woman at that hour. Interestingly, each sculpture is by a different artist, yet they fit together so perfectly as a set.

1. *Dawn.* She is obviously a morning person, ready to take on the day! He... really wants his morning coffee!

Top row: left: *Dawn;* **right:** *Day.* **Bottom row: left:** *Twilight;*
right: *Night*

2. *Day.* I love how hungrily this man with his slingshot
   gulps from the woman's water jug. He pulls her hip into
   him with his free hand, suggesting they are more than

just friends. She seems pretty matter of fact about it, as if quenching his thirst is all about hydration for her... at least in the middle of the day.

3. *Twilight.* This one's my favorite. He's resting on his plow; she's still got a sickle in her hand. A hard day's work in the field is just done and they are tired, but they lean into each other in a way that conveys to me they are totally relaxed in one another's company. I love her elbow on his knee, her head tilted back. But I will say, his thoughts seem far away, on the horizon. Is he thinking about a better life for them, or just annoyed that there's a pigeon on his head?

4. *Night.* He seems to have just arrived home, or perhaps it is she who has been out (he is, after all, naked, except for his cape). In any event, she's delighted to see him, engaging in a little game of "peekaboo" to get his attention. Their faces are so close, the intimacy of her intention is unmistakeable.

***

Parc Monceau is an extravagant "English Garden" in a rather upscale, residential part of Paris. It's got fake Greek ruins, pony rides, a little Chinese bridge, and several very sweet couple statues. I'm only going to feature my favorite two, which Teresa and I discovered on a recent stroll.

The first (below left) struck me as absolutely hilarious. I wanted to title it: "Mansplaining": She really looks as if she has had enough of this older man lecturing her, looking down from his perch on the rock. Her eyes gaze off into the distance, and her hands seem to be shredding something. In fact, this is a statue of the French opera composer and professor of the Conservatoire de Paris, Ambroise Thomas. So, perhaps this young woman is

Left: "Mansplaining," Right: "Honey, you promised to fix the toilet today!"

just one of many who got to listen to him go on and on about music in the course of his long career. ("Lucky *me!*" as Teresa would say).

When Teresa and I first set eyes on this next statue (above right), we agreed it should be titled, "Honey, you promised to fix the toilet today!" The woman looks like she's doing her best to be patient, but now it can't wait any longer. He looks like he's resigned, but would rather do anything else in the world. Look at his legs moving away from the direction in which she's guiding him! Well, perhaps we were projecting? The statue is actually *Alfred Musset and the Muse.* It is based on the author's poem, in which the Muse attempts to pursuade Musset to write. But hey, I've been there too, Alfred, and when words turn to mush on my page, sometimes I would rather go fix the toilet.

***

Posterity consoles Lamarck

Just inside the front gates of the *Jardin des Plantes* on a massive pedestal stands a formidable statue of Jean-Baptiste Lamarck (1744–1829), the great French naturalist who published the first coherent and solidly supported theory of evolution in 1800. Fifty years later, Charles Darwin published *On the Origin of Species,* promoting the theory of Natural Selection as the driving force of evolution, which basically blew Lamarck's version of the theory out of the water. The front of his statue proclaims Lamarck to be the "Founder of the Doctrine of Evolution." On the back of the pedestal is a smaller bronze relief statue of a woman, "Posterity," with her hand lightly, consolingly, on Lamarck's shoulder.

The plaque reads: "La postérité vous admirera, Elle vous vengera, mon père." Translation: "Posterity will admire you, She will avenge you, my father." What I love about this is the expression on his face as he looks up at her. Look at his knees together, his hands on his lap like a school boy at last receiving some praise from the schoolmarm!

***

My favorite couple statue in all Paris is in the *Jardin Luxembourg*. It's a dramatic tableau at the center of the *Medici Fountain,* featuring the famous mythological lovers Acis and Galatea. He was a shepherd youth; she was a nymph, a daughter of the sea-god Poseidon. The lustrous white marble sculpture captures the lovers in a tender embrace, gazing deeply into each other's eyes as if they have just had sex. She seems completely relaxed and happy, her left hand wrapped around his neck, her fingers playing with Acis' hair.

Zooming out, on the rocks just above the unsuspecting pair looms the giant cylops Polyphemus, cast in dark bronze. As Ovid tells the story, Polyphemus was enamoured with Galatea. When he came upon the lovers by the seashore, he became enraged and hurled a boulder at Acis, mortally wounding him. And so this achingly beautiful moment becomes overshadowed by violence...

Because she's a nymph—a water spirit—Galetea had the power to transform Acis' blood into a flowing river just before he died, thus saving his life, though not in his human form. The River Acis flows in Sicily to this day. The myth, stripped to its essence reminds me that life's sweetest moments are fleeting in an unpredictable and sometimes-dangerous world. But also that, like Galetea, we too have agency. We can't undo an act of violence, but we can transform the result, as she transforms Acis blood into a source of life.

***

I hope I have filled your heads with beautiful images of love and care, passion and playfulness, when you contemplate

Acis and Galatea share a tender but fatal moment.

Paris. Maybe you can think about the many ways your body moves in physical space in the dance of relationship with those you cherish. Savor these touches, these gestures, with all your heart.

Part III

Northern Italy

Alpine Flâniker

Chapter 20

Unexpected Lake Como

The one thing everyone seems to knows about Lake Como is that George Clooney has a ten-million-dollar villa on its shore. That factoid fits well with the "Beverley Hills of Italy" impression of the famous lake: glitzy shopping, mansions, high fashion, the playground of the rich and famous. When Teresa decided to book us for a week on the lake at the start of our romp through the Italian Alps, I confessed this did not sound at all like fun to me. She showed me some pictures of colorful old houses clustered by the water, and damn, they looked as beautiful as a painting. Somewhat reluctantly, I was ready to sign up.

We arrived first at Como, the main town at the southern end of the lake. We drove past block after block of nondescript buildings and condos. Congested traffic, people everywhere, noisy. We finally found a parking garage more than a kilometer from the lakefront and joined the throng flowing down towards the old town and the water. Much of this area is a pedestrian zone, but all its charm has been commercialized, with stores and shops from end to end. When we finally reached the lake, we found it lined with hotels and restaurants, including a McDonald's. Como was just as bad as I had feared.

Teresa assured me that Varenna, the town where we were staying for the week, would be different. Varenna was an hour's drive away from Como on the opposite side of the lake. We checked in to our little Airbnb house in the tiny village of Fiumilatte, a short walk away. Our little balcony opened out directly over the lake, with deep blue mountains rising serenely from the water on the far shore.

Varenna, a drone's eye view (my photo of a poster from the Varenna tourism board).

We took a 20-minute stroll into the heart of Varenna and absolutely fell in love with it. From the twelfth-century church in the main square, steep streets dropped to a little beach lined with cute cafés and *gelaterias*. The old houses were painted various shades of red, yellow, pink and tan, with here and there a few stone villas. There was no crass development. It seemed as if the town had not been touched by time. A hanging walkway took us over the water and around a cliff to the tiny ferry terminal on the other side—the only modern structure in town. Looking up, we could see the ruins of an ancient castle on the hilltop. On our walk home in the twilight, I noticed a sign on the outskirts of town from the local tourist board. It read, simply, in English and Italian, "Varenna... the Lake Como you expect."

Next day I climbed the forest path to the castle ruins above the city. It was a safe haven for townfolk in centuries past, when raiding parties from Como used to terrorize them. From the turrets, looking out, one could see across the water and the well to the vast northern part of the lake that was forested with pines and seemed more like northern British Columbia than a glitzy lake resort.

Lake Como turned out to be not at all what I, personally, expected. In fact, I came to see that there were several different Lake Comos. Sure, there was the commercialized, overdeveloped Como in the south. But there was also the authentic beauty of Varenna. It turns out the preservation of so many old houses was due to the extreme poverty of the local villagers more than anything else. They simply could not afford to build new houses. What's most impressive though, is that the citizens grasped the magic of their little town early on and didn't spoil it with haphazard development. We heard they are so determined

Welcome to Villa Monastero

to preserve their inheritance, the owners of houses in the old town can't even change the *color* of their paint.

Varenna also has a few beautiful old villas from earlier centuries, one of which was once also a convent and is now a public garden. *Villa Monastero* evokes a faded splendor of the Italian aristocracy: in the time before roads the nobles would arrive by boat, and so the fountains and statuary all face towards the water to greet them.

There is also the wild Como of the north, dotted with small, working towns that seemed like the Pacific Northwest, but with more pizza. These contained some great hiking trails. One afternoon I took a ferry across the lake to the town of Menaggio. Within half an hour of the ferry terminal I found myself utterly alone in the Parco Val Sanagra. The path wound through a forest of tall fir trees, the ground thick and soft with a carpet of rust-red fallen needles. The trail descended back along a stream strewn with the ruins of old mills and kilns, and an ancient, arched stone bridge. The stream fell into a gorge which cut deep in the mountainside, The route through it was carved out of the sheer rock, and I had to duck to avoid hitting my head. I crossed harrowing walkways as narrow as gangplanks over vertiginous drops, before emerging from the green woods at Menaggio's municipal waterworks on the outskirts of town. If not for the occasional view of a villa on a hillside, I might have been hiking through a B.C. wilderness.

And finally, there is Bellagio, the luxurious heart of the lake where the rich and famous frolic. We took the ferry there one afternoon, ready to be intimidated. But honestly, it was charming. Sure, there were a few high-end hotels, but these were in gorgeous, butter-colored villas. It was not nearly as commercialized as Como. We suppose that today's well-heeled "nobles" keep their extravagance within their gated villas, and don't announce it to the shoreline as in ages past. We traipsed up and down the steep streets of the central shopping district lined with tiny boutiques that oozed quality and authentic old-world charm.

Teresa bought herself a fancy purse, but not some made-in-China Gucci or Prada. The workshop where the purses were made was right below the salesroom. We walked around the building and through the window on the lower floor spied several artisans cutting and stitching leather. They waved enthusiastically at us when we held up Teresa's new purchase for them to see.

By the end of the week, I came to love the many Lake Comos we had explored. I hope we come back to Varenna. If we do, we will return to our little house by the water. As a parting gift one of the owners gave us a little painting she made of the Fiumilatte waterfall. A sweet gesture, from a sweet woman, from a sweet and very special place.

Chapter 21

Riding the Bernina Express

"Do you want to ride the luxury Bernina Express from Tirano in Italy to San Moritz in Switzerland?" I asked. " It's the highest rail pass in Europe."

"You had me at 'luxury,'" replied Teresa, her brown eyes bright with excitement. "Let's go First Class!"

I winced. The skinflint tendencies of my Scottish ancestry bubbled to the surface.

"But that's 300 euros for the both of us!" I sputtered. "Second class is only half that price! The mountains out the window will look exactly the same either way..."

"Look, if I'm going to ride a *luxury express* over the Alps, I'm *not* doing it second class!" said my beloved, eyes now flashing fierce.

In any good marriage there is an expression one learns to read that means, "this is not up for debate." It required a bit of mental jiu-jitsu on my part to concede with grace. I asked myself if I would gladly pay 300 euros for the trip if those were the only tickets available. Well, yes I would. My inner adventurer thus overpowered my inner Scot, and thus I avoided a nasty derailment before we even stepped on board the train.

The Bernina Express is run by the Swiss, which you can tell from the precision of their website. It describes the trip like this:

On the highest railway across the Alps, the Bernina Express climbs up to the glistening glaciers before descending to the palms of Italy far below.... The train negotiates the 55 tunnels, 196 bridges and inclines of up to 70 per mille with ease. At the highest point on the RhB, 2,253 metres above sea level, you will find the Ospizio Bernina. Here, visitors can delight in the cultural and natural surroundings and enjoy the Alps at their most impressive. The railway line from Thusis—Valposchiavo—Tirano has UNESCO World Heritage status. Thanks to the modern panoramic cars, you will enjoy unrestricted views of the unspoilt Alpine panorama.

Wikipedia adds that it is also one of the steepest standard railways in the world, with inclines up to seven percent.

When we boarded our train the next day, the first thing we noticed was that it was a bright, shiny red, like a fire truck, and absolutely immaculate, as one might expect of the Swiss. It had big windows that curved right up to the roof, so you could easily look up at the peaks. Our first-class seats were spread out from each other and comfortable. Plus, there were only two other couples in our entire car. Meanwhile, entire tour groups were shuffling into the second-class compartments and stuffing them full. So the decision to travel first class seemed like a major score for the trip, as we could bounce freely back and forth from side to side, depending on which window had the best view at any given moment.

Unfortunately, one of the other two couples in our car began a long and loud conversation as we pulled out of the station. She was doing most of the talking, explaining at length about how *his* bad attitude was spoiling their trip. She had a hectoring, nasal tone in her voice that grated on our ears. Every now and then he would interject weakly, "but I didn't *do* anything!" Oh, if only we were in a crowded car, where we would not hear them for the chattering masses!

The train climbed up the green valley, and soon crossed the Swiss border. It then reached the first of those wonderous engineering feats, an uphill corkscrew called the Brusio Circular Viaduct. Because the train can't pull itself up too steep an incline, the railway spirals up in an overlapping circle over a viaduct to gain altitude.

We rose to what seemed the top of the valley, but was actually the bottom of the next, higher valley, arriving on the shores of the beautiful aqua-blue Lake Poschiavo. We saw snow-capped mountains at the far end. Was that really where our train was headed? Our car fell silent. There was no more talk of relationships... at least for a while.

We began the steep ride up, up, and up. The train skirted along cliff edges and passed through several tunnels, at times slowing near to a halt as it puffed its way higher and higher. After almost two hours on board, we stopped for a 15-minute break near the pass at Alp Grum Station, 2,019 meters above sea level (from our start at 429 meters at Tirano). We got out to look around at the mineral-green lake, fed by a glacier visible at the end of the valley. The wind carried the chill of ice.

We kept climbing. Soon there was snow on both sides of the track, and we reached the pass at Ospizio Bernina, right next to the glacier-covered Bernina Massif, the highest rail pass in

The Ospizio Bernina Pass

Europe at 2,253 meters. As we rolled through the snowfields, the audio commentary advised to watch for the yellow sign. South of the sign, water flowed into the Adriatic Sea; north of the sign, it flowed to the Black Sea (mostly through the Danube River, I imagine).

Down the other side of this astonishing high-altitude mountain pass, the train dropped about 200 meters and reached St. Moritz surprisingly quickly. In that short time, winter had turned back to spring again: warm and sunny, the trees all green around the little glacial lake. Teresa last visited this little town thirty years ago ("another husband, another lifetime"). She remembered it as a charming chic village full of wooden houses, a few subdued designer shops and a smattering of classy hotels in beautiful Swiss architecture spread alongside the lake: a rustic, classy winter playground of the rich and famous.

But gosh, we were disappointed. Teresa said St. Moritz was not at all as she recalled it. A lot of new concrete hotels and condos crowded round the few remaining old buildings. What was worse for her, at this time of year, between skiing and hiking seasons, the designer shops were all closed.

After a lunch and stroll through the village and lake, it was time to take the train back to Trevino. This time, there was only one other couple on board our luxury first-class car. As we entered, they waved at us, "Hello again!" Our hearts sank. It was the quarrelsome couple from the morning train! But they seemed to have made up in St. Moritz, and the spectacular ride back to Italy was blissfully quiet.

Chapter 22

Bormio's Wild Mountains

Flâneur lesson #13: Flâneuring while hiking equals flâniking

A topographic map of Italy shows large splotches of white around Bormio, a ski-town just south of the Swiss border. The area contains the highest mountains in Italy, including glaciers, snowfields, vast forests, and high mountain passes.

It's packed with skiers in the winter, hikers and mountainbikers in the summer. Except for the month of May, the "dead season," which is when Teresa and I decided to visit. Most of the restaurants, shops and chalets were closed, and the streets of the pedestrian old town were eerily quiet. The "dead season" is why Teresa was able to find a chalet for rent just above the old town with a spectacular view of the peaks that was affordable for a whole week.

My plan for our stay was to get my hiking legs in shape for the summer. My buddy Jim texted me a pointed question: "Can one flâneur in the mountains? Isn't it technically a Paris kind of thing?"

He was, of course, correct. The concept of a "flâneur," as developed in Paris in the late 1800s, was a strictly urban phenomenon. It describes one who wanders the city streets, without a plan, just observing society. There's neither street nor society in the great outdoors. I wrote back to Jim, arguing that with the right attitude, one could flâneur in the woods just as well as along the boulevards:

"I tend to head out for a hike with a vague idea of where I want to go, but only pick a path once I'm there. Yesterday the route I wanted to follow was closed for construction, so I drove

A flâneur contemplates his next flânike in the Italian Alps.

around for a bit, searching for an alternative trailhead. When I found a good place, I literally chose my route at the fork in the road. I ended up not on the path I thought I was choosing, but, oh well, same mountain. So up I went. I think my urban flâneuring has made me a bit more flexible hiking when the unexpected happens."

Indeed, the trail I happened upon that day charmed me because, unlike all the other paths in the area, it had a hand-carved wooden entranceway: "La Romantica." This was not meant to evoke romance, but rather the Romanticism of earlier ages that focused on a love of nature. A wooden signpost marked every bend along this upward winding path. Each sign featured a quote about nature. All in Italian, of course, so I could only get the gist of them. What I loved, though, was that these were not famous writers. They were from hikers from previous years who visited the region and contributed their thoughts. For example, Post #1, by a woman named Virginia: *I Monti sono Maestri muti e fanno Discepoli silenziosi:* "The Mountains are mute Masters and make silent Disciples."

Part of my inspiration for this hybrid of flâneuring and hiking (which I dubbed *flâniking*) comes from another friend, Hank. He and I have hiked and kayaked together, and we are both long-time members of the same men's group. Hank now lives in Mississipi, where he paddles and hikes regularly, vlogging about life, death, and paddling, as he roams the swamplands that he loves so well (see his YouTube channel: *Hank's Deep Thoughts*). Like me, Hank finds being alone in nature connects him to the wholeness of life. In being absorbed into the wilderness, you lose yourself, and can let go of the ego's grasping for immortality. He and I conferred on the issue, and we both agreed one can flâneur in the wild.

I find flâniking through the Italian Alps helps me stay focused on the present moment. The trails are steep enough to keep me paying attention, so my thoughts don't wander for fear of one foot going amiss and me sliding off the edge into the void. At the same time, when I look up at the mountains across so much empty space, that same void evokes a sense of awe and wonder. I recalled the opening lines in William Wordsworth's famous poem: *I wandered lonely as a cloud / That floats on high o'er vales and hills.* Yes, like that. But with fewer daffodils, more fear of death.

One of my best flâniking experiences in Bormio was a walk along a high-altitude service road near the "Bormio 2000" ski lifts located, appropriately, at 2,000 meters above sea level. The dirt road winds round the mountain for several kilometers through forest, where I met not a single soul. Eventually the track ended at a high altitude grazing pasture, dotted with purple crocuses in early spring. There was a small but modern wooden cottage, but it was empty. No people, not even cattle with their tinkling bells this time of year.

Next to the cottage, I found two small, turf-covered buildings that were half dug into the earth, used for storage. They must have been shepherd huts in ages past. These huts connected me for an instant to the people who lived here in earlier eras: Medieval, Roman, and even prehistoric. The earliest remains of settlements further up the valley have been dated to 10,000 years ago. Ötzi, the 5,300-year-old "Ice Man," was discovered freeze-dried and entombed in ice on a mountain pass less than a hundred miles from here.

On my walk back towards the slopes, it started to rain lightly, and the dirt track got a bit muddy. Because I was

Too big for a dog paw!

flâniking, the drizzle didn't cause me to hurry. As I sauntered along, I noticed a bunch of fresh tracks that were not there on my outbound walk when the ground was dry: deer, fox, cat... and then this massive paw print (below) *which was not there two hours earlier:*

I'm not exactly Daniel Boone, but I recognized the shape of the paw as canine. But too big for a dog. With not a single human print on the trail, it was hard to imagine a dog roaming around alone way out here. Could it possibly be a wolf? I walked the final kilometer back to my car, and when I returned to our condo, I emailed the photo above to my friend Chris, a wildlife biologist.

He swiftly replied: "Really interesting. Either a truly large dog, or a wolf. Might want to check if this region of Italy has the latter. They've made quite the comeback in much of that area of Europe..."

I searched online, and found this from a local newspaper. Bear in mind, the hillside were I was hiking was in the same valley as San Gallo. Here's a translation of the article from the Italian:

Spotted a wolf in Bormio, a resident finds it in front of him in the locality of San Gallo, Bormio, November 14, 2019—Singular sighting, complete with video evidence, and now the presence of a wolf in Alta Valtellina is practically certain. A few days ago a mauled sheep was found in the municipal area of Sondalo, the owner immediately thought of a wolf and reported the macabre discovery to the competent authorities. The confirmation of the presence of the animal came thanks to the video posted yesterday on Facebook by a Bormino, who found himself face to face with the splendid specimen, walking quietly on the snow on the side of the roadway in San Gallo in Bormio. In the video you can see the animal walking and, when it noticed the presence of the car, it stops, in favor of the camera, and then resumes its walk.

While it's far from certain that the wolf video-taped in 2019 made the fresh tracks that I saw in 2022, wolves have in fact returned to Bormio, so... wolf tracks in the Alps. That's one thing a flâneur most definitely won't find on the boulevards of Paris.

Chapter 23

The Mighty Dolomiti

Flâneur Lesson #12: Flâmotoring is also a thing

"I'm afraid we have done this trip through north Italy the wrong way round," said Teresa as we were leaving Bormio, heading east to our next destination. "Now that we've seen the highest peaks in Italy—snow caps and glaciers—I'm worried the Dolomites will be anticlimactic."

It doesn't happen very often, but, boy, was my beloved wrong about that one!

We drove down, down, down from the Alps, east along the Adige Valley to Bolzano, the capital of South Tyrol, already humid in mid-May. From there, it was a short, winding, uphill drive to Castelrotto, our home for the next four days. Castelrotto is perched on the edge of the *Alpe di Siusi*, the most eastern part of the *Dolomiti* (as the Italians call the Dolomites

Castelrotto and the Dolomites

mountain range). As we drove into Castelrotto, we rounded a bend and caught our first glimpse of the Dolomites. *Holy Crap!* They seemed to jump right out of the sky in front of us.

The Alpe di Suisi is the largest high alpine meadow in all of Europe, and it is ringed by the Dolomites as if by massive stone guardians. We took a drive up for a peek that first evening. Most of the year, you absolutely, positively cannot do this. The Alpe di Suisi is immensely popular in summer and winter, and so it is closed to car traffic to keep down air pollution and noise. Instead, everyone takes a gondola ride to the little village at the top, Compatsch, and hikes or skis from there. Except for one week of the year in mid-May, which is low season, when the gondolas, restaurants and most of the hotels all close for vacations and repair. That is exactly when we arrived. So we drove up to this most famous high alpine meadow at twilight

This is my best shot of the whole Alpe di Suisi, from a hike I took up to the far rim later in the week. It's not the view from our first drive. Note the Alps way in the background.

on our first day. We found the gates open and ourselves alone in a vast, silent land of rolling green spaces, utterly empty except for us. On the far side of the Alpe di Suisi, we could see an even higher range of Dolomites rise like a jagged wall that hemmed in the eastern cusp of the plateau. It looked as if ancient giants had once built stone ramparts around the meadow to protect it from meddlesome humans, but these had crumbled through the eons, and no longer kept intruders like us away from their lofty domain.

In the days that followed, we explored the valleys around the Alpe de Suisi, driving with only the vaguest of plans, following minor roads up twisting forest ravines just to see where they led. This flâneuring-by-car we dubbed *flâmotoring*. Often we would end up climbing harrowing switchbacks, arriving at stupendous mountain passes with staggering views that took our breath away; eventually I was drained of all descriptive clichès.

One strange thing Teresa and I both experienced was a scared-thrilled feeling as we drove alongside these rocky behemoths. The Dolomites aren't triangular like most mountains. They jutt. They form spires and columns and curtains of stone. When you drive right alongside them, the sheer massive verticality of them is disorienting. It made us feel dizzy. It made us feel afraid.

It turns out this fearsomeness had deep roots. There are indeed many legends about these stone peaks, passed on from generation to generation by those who live in their shadows. One of the most compelling is the story of Tanna, Queen of the Crodères. These are stone beings who live in the peaks and in some sense *are* the peaks as well. Here's the story, which I have condensed from various sources:

Tanna lifted up her head to the sun to warm it, and when her icy hair melted it formed a valley, where trees, grass, and flowers sprouted. They grew into her until her heart began to beat. But, when she tried to embrace her rocky sisters, they rebuffed her, leaving her sad and lonely. She took some earth from her hips and with it created human beings. They climbed up and down the Croderes, tickling them like ants. She was delighted. The other Croderes, however, sent water and mudslides down the valley, burying a lot of people, covering their huts, and destroying their alpine pastures. Tanna protected them as best she could from wind and water with her magic blue stone. She saw how people loved and consoled each other, and wanted to live with them. But the other Croderes said to her, "If you want to do that, you must give us your magic stone, and you cannot remain our queen...."

The story does not end well for Tanna, nor the people she created. They will suffer; many will be crushed by avalanches, including her own son. In the end, when her heart breaks, she turns back into stone. Then Tanna is again the proud queen of the mountains. She rules the vast heights in cold beauty, without sorrow and without love, for she has regained the equanimity of the Croderes.

Geology, of course, tells a different story of the Dolomites, but one no less dramatic:

The characteristic rock of the Dolomites consists of fossilized coral reefs formed during the Triassic Period (around 250 million years ago) by organisms and sedimentary matter at the bottom of the ancient tropical Tethys Ocean. The Alps arose as a result of the collision of the African and European tectonic plates, forcing the rocks at the point of impact to soar skyward. The ocean which formerly divided these two continents disappeared, and the Dolomites became mountains.

—South Tyrol Info website

That's right. The Dolomites are the remains of coral reefs, sculpted by earthquakes, volcanic eruptions, wind, ice and rain for millions of years. But wait a minute: limestone is relatively soft (remember the Sponge-taffy cliffs of the Algarve?). So what makes the Dolomites hard enough that they could endure all that pounding from the elements? Think of a coral shell, which is primarily calcium. Stacked up hundreds of feet, under tremendous pressure and over geological eras, the coral mineralizes into calcium magnesium carbonate: a pale, hard, mineral that looks almost chalk-like. In fact, the Dolomites were historically known as the *Monti Pallidi*—Pale Moutains—until French geologist Déodat de Dolomieu (1750–1801) came along. He made the first scientific study of these mountains and their mineral composition, and so today, both the mineral and the mountains bear his name.

On one of our drives, Teresa and I stopped at Lake Caressa. The Latemar Massif, right behind the small lake, is in fact an entire coral atoll that grew up to 500 meters in the ancient sea

The Latemar Massif and the "Procession of the Dolls."

bed. The spires of the massif are known as the "Procession of the Dolls." An old legend says they were once enchanted dolls belonging to a magician that were turned to stone by a witch's curse.

Another legend says that the many shimmering colors on the lake are the result of a sorcerer's plot to catch the Nymph of the Lake by luring her out into the open with a rainbow. But the nymph escaped his trap, and in a fit of anger he threw the rainbow into the water where it dissolved. If I were to write a legend, it would be of the Latemar Dolomites gazing into this pool at their feet, and remembering their birth from living coral, 250 million years ago, in a vast and shallow sea.

It's often said that the vastness of mountains can make people feel small. I find the timescale of the Dolomites makes me feel not only tiny, but also temporary. My life is the briefest flicker compared to their unfolding story, which may well last hundreds of millions years more. Yet as Teresa and I flâmotor among them, I don't feel insignificant. It feels so wondrous that a tiny spark like me can be here, like a little ant tickling the Crodères as I crawl through their domain; that I can take all the vastness of them in with my senses, and respond with fear and awe. Because of this, even when I leave, I know the mighty Dolomiti will stay inside of me.

Chapter 24

Encountering the "Wild Man"

Since Teresa and I arrived in Lombardy three weeks ago, we have had three encounters with Italy's *l'Homo Salvadego*, the "Wild Man." These hairy, human-like creatures are a European counterpart to Big Foot, Yeti, and the Vietnamese *Nguoi Rung* ("People of the Forest"). In the town of Sondalo, we drove past a bizarre statue (below left) about ten feet tall on somebody's lawn, right by the roadside. There was no sign or anything to explain this seemingly crazy bit of art. Indeed, we might have passed by without even paying attention if not for an attempt a few days earlier to find a fresco of a Wild Man I had read about in the nearby mountain village of Sacco. The Sacco *Museo dell'Homo Salvadego* is housed in a fifteenth-century wooden

Wild Man on a lawn in Sonaldo (left), and on a wall in Sacco (right).

building, and the fresco itself is painted on an interior wall (below right).

The Wild Man of Sacco is shown carrying a club. He is bearded and covered in hair except for his face, feet, hands and genitals. The inscription next to him reads: *Ego sonto un homo salvadego per natura, chi me ofende ge fo pagura.* In translation: "I'm a wild man by nature, those who offend me I will put fear."

A little research showed that the Wild Man appears in many places in Europe's late Medieval art: in statues, woodcuts, paintings, even coats of arms. He was always bearded, his body covered with thick dark hair, and invariably he carries a club. I remembered from earlier visits to the continent that such a figure is part of many pre-Christian festivals that continue to this day in mountainous and rural parts of Europe, from Iberia to Scandinavia. Usually, these costumed characters also carry a club or staff like the one in the Sacco fresco.

Our third encounter took place in the Dolomites, by the shore of Lake Carezza, where the local park service has put up a series of informative plaques, some of which retell the traditional legends of the region. One of these told the story of the Wild Men of the Latemar, which I have transcribed:

Clans of wild men used to eke out a meagre existence around Lake Carezza. Up above in the mountains lived shy dwarves, while the occasional giant would come by and settle with the wild men, sometimes marrying their daughters… Then new dwellers, the Dirlingers, moved into the valley, and peace became a thing of the past. The farmers wanted to use the pastures and the forest but the wild men would not let them. No one heeded the warnings of the ancients on either side, and so the inevitable happened: a terrible war broke out between the old inhabitants and the newcomers, and no courage, strength or bravery, not even the help of the dwarves, could prevent all of the Latemar wild men from being slain…

So, what's the origin of this mysterious, ubiquitous, hirsute figure? There are three main hypotheses:

1. Wild Men are really cases of *hypertrichosis—a* genetic mutation that causes hair to grow all over a person's body. It's easy to imagine people with this mutation being shunned by village society and forced to live in the forests. But hypertrichosis typically covers the full face and extremities, including the forehead, unlike the Medieval Wild Man. Cases of hypertrichosis have also been reported in medieval times, and these are not confused with Wild Men. I think it would be hard to explain how this mutation could become a figure in festivals across the continent, or turn into a legend about a whole race of creatures.

2. Wild Men are *mythological figures*, perhaps akin to giants, werewolves, and other scary monsters that populate European folklore. This is certainly plausible, though it begs the question of how such a similar creature evolved from very different mythological traditions from Asia to North America.

3. Wild Men have a *basis in fac*t. Specifically, they are trace memories of Neanderthals, from the period when our two species coexisted in Europe. Current science dates the most recent fossil evidence of Neanderthals at approximately 24,000 B.C. That is about 1,250 generations. A long, long time for folk memories to persist! But, of course, only about 300 Neanderthal skeletons have been found to date. They existed for about 350,000 years, so that extinction date is simply all we can guess from a very tiny sample size.

Pockets of survivors could perhaps have existed much, much later, explaining the persistence of the legends, and perhaps the more recent sightings of Yeti-like creatures in various remote parts of the planet. Of course, if the Wild Men are based on real creatures, then they are more accurately Wild Men and Wild Women—the Latemar legend talks specifically about their *daughters*. (Indeed, there are stories and depictions of wild women, but these are significantly more rare.)

I found a really interesting argument for this last idea in a research paper by Olivier Décobert, published in the *Relict Hominoid Inquiry* (4:37–52, 2015). His essay includes accounts of historical sightings of Wild Men, including one from "a French engineer Julien David Leroy, who wrote in his work on logging in the mountains of the Pyrenees that in 1774, the pastors of the Iraty Forest (region of Saint-Jean-Pied-de-Port) often saw a Wildman, described as shaggy like a bear." Décobert also describes a 1988 account of a shepherd who claimed to have observed a Wild Man in the mountains of Pakistan for two hours, and drew a remarkably Neanderthal-like sketch of the creature.

If you think it's impossible Neanderthals could have survived for thousands of years undetected, then such accounts won't likely convince you. However, it's a suprisingly common occurrence that species thought to be extinct are rediscovered (see the book *Woody's Last Laugh* for a riveting and humorous account of how the supposed extinction of the Ivory Billed Woodpecker bedevils scientists to this day).

While my imagination loves the idea that Neanderthals might still be with us, living undetected in the remote Italian Alps and other wild places, my rational mind thinks that's highly improbable. But it's not at all implausible that small, wary groups could have lingered in these hills into historical times, long enough that *Homo sapiens* remembered them, and immortalized our genetic next-of-kin in art, ritual and legend.

Intriguingly, recent genetic research has revealed that Neanderthal DNA lingers on in *Homo sapiens*. On average about 3% of our genes were inherited from Neanderthal ancestors. So, they were more than just prehistoric neighbors. We interbred. Whether it was climate change, lack of genetic diversity, or conflict with us that finally drove Neanderthals to extinction, they persist more than in our imagination. We each have some of the Wild Man or Wild Woman in us. I wonder if that is what draws me to their memory, as I flâneur through these alpine forests and peaks that were once their home.

Chapter 25

Would My Death Be Tragedy or Stupidity?

A perfect day for flâniking. Sunshine. Blue sky. The pale peaks of the Dolomites calling my name. Teresa was happily ensconced in our 150-year-old Tyrolian hotel at Lago de Braies, in the far north of Italy. So I headed off for a trail that my hiking app described as "challenging." It would take me from the lakeside through the forest and up to the enticing nearby peaks — peaks that I could see from our hotel balcony.

An hour later, I found myself scrambling up a ravine of white dolomite scree right to the base of Herrstein Mountain — literally, "Mr. Stone Mountain." A crevice in the side of the rock was still packed with snow, the last traces of winter on this warm spring day. Standing in this spot, looking up the sheer side of Mr. Stone gave me a fearful sense of vertigo, as if my mind could not quite grasp what it was seeing and simply flooded my body with adrenaline and danger signals. I caught my breath and pushed on up the slope to where the trail hugged the cliffside. It dropped precipitously on the other side.

I'd been on perhaps a dozen mountain hikes in the past three weeks. My legs were getting strong, my lungs accustomed to the altitude. I was feeling pretty good for a man pushing 64. But the path ahead scared me. Mentally, I envisioned what would happen if I slipped. There was some scrubby vegetation by the edge of the path, a fir bush here and there. But mostly it was loose dolomite scree falling away at what looked to be a 60-degree angle. Nothing would slow the trajectory of a tumbling man. I would slide straight down. If lucky, I might crash into a fallen log or protruding rock, and bounce once or twice before careening over a vertical drop. The bottom, I could not see. I steeled myself, picked my next resting point, and kept my eyes on the path until I reached that spot. Then I picked another. I promised myself I would turn back if it got too much for me. I made it about half a kilometer this way. I could see the path ahead was only getting steeper.

Honestly, it's not that the trail was unsafe. There was enough room to walk. But no margin for error. My problem was that a few years ago I tore the meniscus in my left knee. I had to give up running, and for a while even walking was painful. I've rehabbed and exercised it back into shape, but every now and then, I feel a twinge in the hinge, and I don't fully trust it. With every step, I thought of that knee. And I knew that when I turned around, climbing down the path would be more jarring, and it would be harder to recover if the knee buckled.

I sat down to rest and just took in the spectacular view. Suddenly, I heard the awful sound of a falling rock, something sliding through the shale below me. It was down to my left. I turned and glimpsed a tawny, horned, four-legged creature running *down* the steep slope. It was a chamois. Damn, the little goat-antelope was running on scree where I would have been be pitifully tumbling. I cursed its four nimble feet.

Of course, I should have brought an extra pair of legs of my own. I should have brought some hiking poles. I didn't even think about it, though I am sure I could have borrowed some from the hotel. Why not? Well, I don't like hiking poles. I like to hike with my hands free.

As I sat and pondered my options, a man appeared far ahead, walking the trail in the opposite direction from me. He was alone, like me. He was in his sixties, like me (so I guessed from his white hair). And, he was striding confidently along with a pair of hiking poles. Not. Like. Me.

It hit me at that moment that if I slipped and skittered down the slope to my death, this would not be considered tragic. On learning about the incident, I could imagine what people would say: "Why the fuck didn't he have hiking poles? Oh, he liked to keep his hands free… and you say he had a bum knee?"

The Italian police report would summarize it thus: "Causa della morte: *stupidità*."

That's the moment I decided to turn around and slowly make my way back down. But I will keep this rare moment of wisdom in mind, and add it to my treasure of advice for other mature flâneurs, whether they amble on concrete or dolomite:

If you died doing what you are about to do, would your death be considered tragedy or stupidity?

Chapter 26

Fresco Frenzy in Castelrotto

We came to Castelrotto in South Tyrol for the spectacular views of the Dolomites mountains. But we never expected to be so charmed by the town itself. Many of Castelrotto's building façades are covered with gorgeous frescos, so that a stroll through the old town is like a visit to an art gallery.

How did this happen? It came down to one native son, Eduard Burgauner. He was a painter of murals in the early 1900s who became obsessed with making Castelrotto one of South Tyrol's most frescoed villages.

A fresco-covered house in Castelrotto.

Before I tell his story, it's worth mentioning that Italy's autonomous province of South Tryol is itself one of the most beautiful regions we have seen in Europe. It's not just the pale-white pinnacles of the Dolomites, the aqua-blue mineral lakes and the chartreuse-green alpine meadows. It's also the care and pride the inhabitants take in making their homes look beautiful—homes that are distinctly different than what we have seen elsewhere in the Italian Alps. And why is that? Because until one hundred years ago, South Tyrol was part of Austria. German is still the most common tongue in the region, and their way of life is more similar to what you might find in Innsbruck, to the north, than in Venice, to the south.

You see, Italy fought with the Allies in WWI, while Austria fought with Germany. In fact, the region is filled with monuments to the many battles waged in the Dolomites 100 years ago. In the aftermath, victorious Italy took South Tyrol as its spoils of war.

You can imagine how uneasy this arrangement was for the region's German speakers—about 70% of today's population of half a million. In 1992, however, South Tyrol negotiated significant autonomy with the Italian government, ending 50 years of dispute. The region now manages their own domestic affairs, including education, health, and tourism. The latter is a big deal. As the province's website puts it, "Tourism is the horse that pulls the South Tyrolean cart." Between hiking and biking in the summer and skiing in the winter, they have six million tourist visitors every year. Their prosperity shows in Castelrotto by how meticulously they maintain the artwork on their houses.

To our great good fortune, Teresa happened to book our stay in Castelrotto at the Hotel Zum Wolf, one of the town's most painted buildings. Their website explains:

The witty frescoes on the façade of the hotel are well known to all visitors of Kastelruth. The author of the frescoes... Eduard Burgauner, was born in a bakers' family on 14th February 1873.... After living in Innsbruck, Memmingen and Vienna, Eduard Burgauner returned to Kastelruth probably at the end of 1901 or the beginning of 1902, at the age of 29. He immediately started working on his ambitious plan to turn Kastelruth into one of South Tyrol's most frescoed villages... The frescoes on the façade of Hotel Zum Wolf were painted in 1907.

The pictures—Jesus and Mary, saints, angels, a butcher, a cat, some beer-swilling drinkers—are complemented by a few verses composed by artist (as translated on the hotel website):

Hotel Zum Wolf's frescoed façade.

For ham and roast
You'll find a good host
A hearty sausage goes down well
with a mug of thirst-quenching ale

and:

Drinking is what a man learns first
Before eating always comes thirst
A good Christian who likes to think
Should never forget the value of drink

Of course, Burgauner was embellishing an age-old tradition of these mountain villages. Teresa and I had noticed many of these distinctive wall paintings since leaving Lake Como. We found out that one of the reasons for painting frescos above doorways was to identify houses. Before streets had names and numbers, (and before most villagers could read), your fresco was your address, as in: "Look for the house with the Archangel Michael killing the dragon."

What I loved about these frescos was their authenticity. Their meticulous conservation reveals the communities' pride in their culture. When a culture gets absorbed by a larger state and becomes a minority, it either loses its identity or holds to it even more fiercely. This might also explain the repeated motifs of families working and playing together, as if to declare, "Look at us, see us for who we are!"

I'm glad the people of South Tyrol have found their place in modern Europe, with genuine autonomy. The creation of a European Union where people can move freely from state to state has been a boon for "nations within states," such as South Tyrol, allowing their cultures to thrive. (This is far from universal, of course, as some minorities in Europe continue to be marginalized: the Roma for instance.)

To me the writing's on the wall—right alongside the frescos, which are much more than a façade. Respecting cultural minorities' rights to self-governance and self-expression is the way to the future. It also points a way for humanity to avoid a globalized monoculture. People cherish their unique cultural identities and need to express them. I want us to be able to revel in our differences. Our common humanity is all the richer for them.

Chapter 27

Ötzi "The Iceman" and Me

One of the most joyful experiences of my life is climbing to the crest of a mountain pass and looking out across a horizon of new peaks and valleys. I've done this again and again during the month Teresa and I have spent in the Italian Alps and Dolomites. I wonder how universal is this sense of awe and beauty that I feel. Did early Europeans experience this? Did Ötzi feel it, just before he died on a remote alpine pass?

The whole world was electrified in 1991 when it was announced that a body found on a remote mountain pass between Italy and Austria was not a lost hiker, as first supposed. Instead, it was the mummified corpse of a man from the Copper Age who had been preserved in a glacier for 5,300 years. Like a time traveler from the deep past, the man nicknamed "Ötzi" brought to the present day not just his well-preserved body, but a treasure trove of artifacts that changed scientists' assumptions about how people lived five millennia ago.

How come he was so well preserved? There was actually less glaciation in the Alps back then. When Ötzi died, he was not immediately covered in ice. Instead he was freeze-dried in the arid, cold climate. It sucked all the moisture out of him like a preserved Parma ham. Gradually glaciation increased, entombing his withered remains in ice and turning him into a natural mummy. And there he lay for five millennia, until the ice retreated, exposing enough of him that a pair of alpine hikers saw something human-like protruding from the ice and they called the police.

Since then, Ötzi has been examined by doctors, dentists, scientists and forensic experts. He has been X-rayed, MRI-ed, carbon-dated. His genome has been mapped and his belongings catalogued and scrutinized in microscopic detail. Even the feces in his colon has been analyzed (sorry, pun intended). The man, and the wealth of information he has to share with us, are now all on display at a special Ice Man Museum that is part of the South Tyrol Museum of Archeology in the provincial capital, Bolzano. So that's where Teresa and I went, to pay our respects.

Here he is, as reconstructed by the museum, Instagram ready (below).

You can't take photos of Ötzi's *actual* remains, but you can view him through a small glass window in his frozen chamber at the museum, which we did. He lies on his back, his smooth taut skin the color of honey. He's a mummy, unbandaged, which makes him seem awfully naked. His left arm is thrown

Ötzi the Iceman

oddly straight across his chest. He's covered in a thin sheen of carefully-maintained ice.

It's a strange, queasy feeling, to look upon a shrivelled yellow-leather thing that was once a human being in some sterile scientific peep show. Surprisingly, I found myself feeling grateful. Ötzi, you have given us so much. Maybe he deserves more dignity than this? But research continues. A few times a year they pull him out of the freezer for new tests and samples, aware that each time he thaws, he turns to mush a little bit more.

So, what do Ötzi and I have in common?

Ötzi was about 45 years of age when he died — an old man for his time, but not so old he could not walk many miles through the mountains. His legs show remarkable musculature. I'm 63, with skinny legs, but in terms of wear and tear, we probably seem about the same age. And, while he's the *Iceman*, I recently discovered that I'm a *SNOWman* (a "woke" acronym I learned recently that stands for "Straight Northern Old White Man").

Ötzi's medical check-up revealed a list of complaints I could relate to: He had mild osteoarthritis in his back, right shoulder and ankle. His right knee has a damaged meniscus (my damage is on the left). But lucky for him he carried two lumps of birch polyphore, a fungus which has anti-inflammatory properties. Me, I carry Advil.

Ötzi's genetic map showed he had the gene for lactose intolerance (he shares that with Teresa). His clothes contained the remains of deer lice and a human flea (currently I'm vermin free, but have been bitten by both). Whipworm eggs were found in his colon, which would have caused abdominal pain and diarrhoea (hookworm for me, once upon a time).

Interestingly enough, his skin bore tattoo marks in patterns that match today's acupuncture charts. So it looks like he was receiving treatment for some of his ailments. Accupuncture and tattoos: check and check for me.

Perhaps even more interesting was the gear Ötzi traveled with across the Alps. There's no way I could go into all the detail of what he was wearing and carrying. Let's just say he was fully self-sustaining, yet able to travel light. What I found most entrancing were his clothes: bear fur hat, deer-and-goat fur leggings, and boots insulated with dried grass to prevent frostbite.

Ötzi also carried a copper-headed axe with a yew handle—the only fully intact axe ever recovered from his time period, for the simple reason that wood disintegrates over thousands of years. But Ötzi's handle was freeze-dried with him. Since there's no evidence that copper was mined in South Tyrol at that time, researchers believed the axehead came from somewhere else (probably southern Tuscany or the Balkans). So the axe is evidence of trade between different regions of Europe in prehistoric times. He also carried a flint knife with a sheath, a quiver of arrows, and an unfinished longbow that presumably he was working on with his knife.

Trapped in his clothing, the earliest known kernels of cereal grain were found; and near his body, a dried sloeberry was discovered—a source of vitamins and minerals that could have served as a prehistoric multivitamin pill. Ötzi seemed prepared for anything.

And so the question arose, why did this intrepid traveler die on this remote mountain pass? For a long time the answer eluded researchers. Then, in an X-ray of Ötzi's chest someone noticed an arrowhead buried just beneath his left shoulder, and subsequently an entry wound in his back. The arrow would have severed the artery to his arm, and he would have swiftly bled to death. From the wound, it was clear he was shot from behind. Ötzi was murdered on that remote mountain pass.

A deep gash was also found in his right hand, which forensic experts determined must have been made several hours before he died. There was also blood on his clothes that was not his own. And so the picture that emerged was of a violent struggle from which Ötzi escaped, perhaps fleeing to the pass hoping to outrun his attacker/s. Because the killer/s left so many valuable items on the corpse, the crime was clearly not a robbery. Most likely, the hit was personal.

It makes me wonder what Ötzi's last moments were like as he ascended that pass. Did he see that new vista on the other side, and, believing he made it to safety, pause for breath? Was he enraptured by the beauty of the mountains ahead of him, and for a second did stand still on the crest, as I would have done, to take in the grandeur—and make himself an easy target? I would like to think the end came swiftly, and that before he was struck, a smile graced his lips in that high, cold place.

That is how I would like to die, when my time comes. Sudden as an arrow, surrounded by mountains. Maybe this is why I feel such a sense of kinship with Ötzi the Iceman.

Chapter 28

Eye to Eye with an Ibex

The ibex looked me right in the eye. He was not in the least bit afraid. After all, he was armed with two giant scimitar horns on his head. And I was on his home turf, quite literally, in Vanoise National Park on the border with Italy, which was created specifically to protect ibex in the French Alps.

I had just rounded a bend in the trail and come across him and his four compadres grazing by the side of the path, as close as if they were playing across from me on a tennis court. I stopped. They moved on slowly. I hiked up above the path a bit to give them some space. The lead male moved ahead, crossing the trail to get above me. For a couple of hundred yards he and

You would not want to butt heads with this guy!

I sauntered parallel to each other along the slope, stopping now and then to take a look at one another. Just two old goats on an alpine hill.

I later learned that alpine ibex typically don't show fear of humans. When confronted with danger, rather than run away, they climb higher. Their ability to cling to steep cliffs is their superpower against predators, so the kind of skittishness you find in deer and other herbivores is not in their nature. This, literally, was part of the ibex's downfall.

Humans and ibex have co-existed in the Alps for more than ten thousand years. In fact, the stomach contents of Ötzi the Iceman revealed that his last meal before he died 5,300 years ago was ibex meat. Ibex are tasty, but they are also nimble, and once on the cliffs no one could catch them. The balance changed though, as human populations increased in the Alps during the Medieval Age, when even high meadows became summer pastures for sheep, cattle, and their hungry herders.

But what really screwed the ibex was the invention of the hunting rifle. Cliffs no longer kept them relatively safe. Instead, cliffs made them sitting ducks. In the nineteenth century the ibex was extirpated in Austria, Germany, Switzerland, Slovenia and Liechtenstein, until fewer than 100 alpine ibex remained alive in the entire world.

Fortunately, in 1856 the Italian king, Vittorio Emmanuelle II, created the Royal Reserve of the Gran Paradiso. Aware of the decline, the king wanted to protect the ibex *from other people* so that he could hunt the remaining ones himself. In his lifetime the king's hunting parties slaughtered thousands of the creatures, and he decorated his palace with hundreds of their majestic horns. What a sicko. And yet, he could not kill them all. Perversely, the king's psychotic drive to murder these beautiful, harmless creatures, combined with his narcissistic need to keep them all for himself, led to the ibex's salvation.

Most of the tourist websites in the region then go on like this: "So, thanks to the creation of the Grand Paradiso Reserve"... *yada yada yada*... "today ibex populations have recovered!" But I found one source, Professor Daniel Croll of the University of Neuchatel, who provides a more detailed and interesting version of the story, (published in EcoEvoCommunity.nature. com):

At the dawn of the 20th century, two ingenious Swiss with the help of an Italian poacher sneaked into the [Gran Paradiso] park and smuggled three younglings over the border to Switzerland. The animals reproduced well in local zoos and soon more individuals were smuggled across the border. In 1911, the first population was reintroduced in the Swiss Alps, followed by many more. Careful planning dictated a very specific reintroduction scheme, with individuals from certain well-established populations being translocated to not yet populated areas. The consequences are not only that the species survived but that Alpine ibex represent one of the best documented, successful species reintroductions...

In 1922, the Royal Reserve of the Gran Paradiso became an Italian National Park. Across the border in France, the Vanoise National Park was created in 1963, with the ibex as its emblem.

In the past 100 years, the ibex population has bounced back to an estimated 5,300 animals across much of its former range. Ibex bring not only massive tourism benefits to the region— indeed, being in their presence was utterly thrilling—they also play an important role in balancing the alpine ecosystems that are their home. For example, their grazing helps spread the seeds of plants and flowers, and their feces adds nutrients to the thin soil.

Today, the alpine ibex is listed as a "species of least concern" by the International Union for Conservation of Nature. In fact, it is the only one of six ibex species in the world that is *not* directly threatened with extinction. The biggest risk to their long-term survival now is inbreeding, which can concentrate unhealthy mutations. Since today's population all sprang from the same 100 animals, that genetic "bottleneck" could still be their ruin. You might think they could breed with other ibex species and diversify their genes. But sadly, attempts at this have failed. Other potentially compatible ibex species live at lower altitudes, and crossbred offspring perished when they were born in the alpine ibex's high ranges.

What has been effective in reducing harmful mutations is breeding new populations with the original group from Gran Paradisio, rather than with other reintroduced groups from Austria, Germany, etc. That's because the Gran Paradisio ibex have the entire range of their remaining original gene pool, whereas reintroduced populations in other countries came from fewer individuals and so they have less genetic diversity. Damn, scientists are smart to figure that out.

It's worth noting that while France, Italy, Swizterland and Germany have banned ibex hunting, appallingly, Austria, Slovenia and Bulgaria still allow it. One hunting website proclaims: "The Alpine Ibex is one of the most exclusive Big Game species that can be hunted in the Alps. Moreover, it is also *the most rare of all Ibex species worldwide to be hunted*." [italic mine.] Shameful!

The ibex and I parted ways as I hiked up to a high alpine lake, *Lac Blanc.* I was all alone. The vista took my breath away. Glaciers in the shadows of the snow-covered peaks. Cascading waterfalls streaming off the precipices. Impossibly high green slopes, littered with massive boulders. As my eyes wandered across that distant wilderness, I suddenly noticed first one, then two regular oblong shapes... holy crap, those are buildings! Probably summer shelters for those tending sheep and cattle. My eyes found a thin path winding up from the village on the valley floor. I guess people are everywhere.

I sat by the lake and ate an orange. This was my final hike in the Alps after five weeks flâneuring and flâniking among them. I had seen a chamois, a few red deer, and even come across some fresh wolf tracks, but I had resigned myself to missing the elusive ibex. What a gift this last day has been, on this green mountainside.

My homeward trail led around the lake and up to a summer hikers' refuge on a hilltop, fronted by a field of purple wildflowers. Just beyond, as the path turned and descended, I heard the skittering of feet on shale, and then a loud snort like a blast from a shrieking kazoo. I started back and saw a large male ibex right below me, trotting away. He had been resting in the shade next to the trail when I startled him. I guess that's one thing an ibex must hate—someone sneaking up on him from above.

Having gained some distance, and recovered his poise, the ibex turned around and looked back at me. Scornfully cool, he moved his massive head from side to side as if daring me to post his charismatic features on social media.

His horns were much longer than the ibex I had seen lower down the mountain. Male ibex's horns grow throughout their lifetimes. That means you can tell who is the oldest by the length of horn, and the male with the longest horns is considered dominant by the other males. So this one was clearly king of the hill. His body was bigger, too. His shaggy winter coat had not yet molted and he looked kind of rough. Ibex can be dangerous if you startle them. But this guy clearly got it that I meant no harm. I'm sure he has seen hikers often enough to know we are no threat. In fact, I bet never once in his long-horned life had he witnessed a person fire a gun at one of his kind. He's safer than an American.

The lucky goat.

Part IV

Norway

Arctic Flâneur

Chapter 29

The Saga of the Electric Car and the Flummoxed Flâneur

"Are you really, really, *really* sure this is a good idea?" Teresa asked, for perhaps the twenty-third time in a tone that made it clear she thought it was a really, really, *really* bad idea.

"Look, this is important to me," I replied to my beloved. "I know that it's going to be an extra hassle, but Norway has the best electric vehicle infrastructure in the world, with literally thousands of charging stations. Eighty-three percent of new cars sold in the country are electric. We can do this. What with climate change and all, if we *can* do it in an EV, then I feel strongly that we *should* do it in an EV."

Thus spoke the old dog, announcing his intention to master a whole new set of tricks.

Silently, Teresa acquiesced. This is not the same as "agreed." I could tell that my statisitics changed her mind not one bit. Norway has been our dream trip since before Covid, and here we were on the cusp of it. So I could understand how she did not want it to be ruined by a car that was not up to the task. But, she was ready to take the course of greatest catastrophe with me, because, well, she loves me so much. She could tell that on this matter, I wanted this, and that I would be hard to budge.

The main issue, of course, was *range anxiety*—the fear of running out of power on the road. The electric vehicle I had booked at the Sixt rental agency in Copenhagen was a Renault with a range of 360 km or so—about 210 miles. We would be driving between 8,000–10,000 kilometers all told from Denmark up the entire length of Norway to the Arctic Circle and back again in 77 days. Much of it would be through sparsely populated areas, where roads wind around fjords, distances between villages are long, and charging stations are few and far between.

The morning we arrived at Sixt, there was no Renault in sight. The EV they gave us instead had a range of only 313 km. About 150 miles! That we could not accept. We put up a fuss. In the end, they agreed to upgrade us to the only other EV they had available: a Polestar 2.

Now, I had never heard of a Polestar. But Teresa's eyes lit up when she heard the name. Polestar is a luxury EV-only carmaker co-owned by Volvo and Geely (a Chinese company). The Polestar 2 is their flagship sedan, touted as a rival to Tesla. The range, the Sixt agent told me, would be 480 km on a full charge! We both said yes.

Business Insider's review says the Polestar 2 is better than a Tesla Model 3: "The interior is built to be something an actual human would use and enjoy—not a button-free, avant-garde exercise in alternative design... it drives like a *finished* version of the Model 3."

Never in my penny-pinching life have I driven such a car, let alone rented one for *two and a half months!* As we glided silently and gently over the bridge from Denmark into Sweden, Teresa suddenly began to talk animatedly about how if we were to ever buy a car again, of course, the only kind that would make sense would be an EV, what with climate change and all...

"The universe loves me," she said, smiling, snuggling into the gorgeously ergonomic seats with more controls than we knew what to do with.

Two hours into our drive, the power was down to less than 10%. What the hell? It was 70% when picked the car up. At this rate, we would be getting no more than... I did the math... 350 km per full charge. But worse, at the first charging station I discovered this magnificent car would not charge above 80%, so we could only top up to 290 km max—a measly 175 miles.

We spent about an hour and a half getting our first charge. We had to wait for another car to finish before we could even start. Then I had trouble with the mobile charging app you need to use to make a purchase. And there were three different kinds of chargers. How could I tell which one to use? The instructions were only in Swedish. I grappled with the electric hose, and finally found the right way to insert the right plug into the slot in the car.

The old dog was feeling like a hangdog by the time were we back on the road.

Our overnight stop on the way to Oslo was the Swedish city of Gothenburg. We checked into the hotel and I called the Sixt rental office and harangued the poor Danish agent. Fortunately, he remained polite and helpful. He told me how I could manually remove the 80% charging limit, which brought us back up to 350 km/charge—doable for the trip, but still only two thirds of what the car was supposedly capable of. Sixt had given us no briefing at all on the vehicle before we drove off. I wondered what else we could perhaps do to increase our range. On the Polestar website I discovered that their international global world headquarters was in... Gothenburg, Sweden, literally a 20-minute drive away from our hotel. Well, we might as well drop round and ask for help.

So next morning, we ambled into Polestar international global world headquarters, told them about our impending Arctic adventure, our utter lack of knowledge about the car, and asked if anyone could offer some advice. The bemused Polestar woman who greeted us grinned widely.

"I'll see if I can find someone to help you," she said.

Five minutes later, Teresa and I were having coffee with Polestar's head of product development, a lovely Swedish woman named Beatrice. She was, indeed, very helpful. She told us first that the 350 km-per-charge range we saw on our

Two flâneurs at Polestar global HQ

dashboard could be low because the previous driver might have been speeding. The car estimates range based on past performance. Since our car only had 1,000 km on it, one reckless previous driver could have skewed the predicted range lower.

That gave us great incentive to drive in a way that maximized our range. But how to do that? Beatrice offered us some great advice:

- Turn off the A/C
- In cold weather, you can set the climate control timer to warm the interior while still charging. That avoids using the battery to heat a cold car as soon as you start driving.

- Don't speed. Going over 130 km/hr (75 mph) drains the battery quickly… and 70–90 km/hour (about 40-55 mph) is optimal.
- When city driving, switch to the *one pedal mode*: You only press on the accelerator. When you take your foot off, the car brakes automatically. This reduces power used for frequent starts-and-stops of city driving.

Beatrice also told us the "official" range for EVs is determined under optimum driving conditions, which no car actually gets in the real world. Well, I suppose the same is true for gas guzzlers too. Damn! If we had ended up in our original car instead of the Polestar, we would likely have had less than a 300 km actual driving range. When we waved goodbye, Teresa and I were not free of range anxiety, but we realized it could have been much worse.

In Oslo that evening we met up with Roald, a dear Norwegian friend whom we have not seen in years. He drove us up to a Holmenkollen Hill, overlooking Oslo. At the top there is an Olympic ski jump—used for zip lines in the summer. We told him about our plan.

"Why an EV?!" he responded.

Teresa maintains he then used the word "crazy."

However, Roald also owns an EV. He told us he's going to drive it to his hometown in the far north in July, so we made plans to meet up. How bad can it be if he's doing it himself? He then told us about a popular YouTube video of a Norwegian man taking a Polestar 2 from Oslo to the Arctic Circle and back. So, not impossible? We found the video, which was uploaded in April 2022, just two months before our trip. The driver, Bjørn Nyland, drove through winter conditions full of ice and snow, in much worse conditions than we would face. His video closed with a great conclusion: "This Polestar was built for this shit. It can handle it fine."

The Polestar might be "built for this shit," but what about your two mature flâneurs? Are we built for it? Will we run out of power in the middle of the Arctic wilderness, and watch the midnight sun wheel round our heads? Will Teresa, Cassandra-like, sit silently in the ergonomic seat next to me, rending her garments, "I told you so" *emanating* from her every pore? The old dog whimpers at the thought.

Chapter 30

The Forces That Formed the Fjords

Flâneur lesson #13: Embrace the awe

Just west of Oslo, civilization disappears. In most countries I know, you go from city to suburb to farmland to wilderness, and in all too many places, the wild spaces in between have been squeezed out altogether. However, leaving Norway's capital for the western fjords, Teresa and I found ourselves in forest before we knew it. We drove past little lakes with a few cottages on them, and when occasionally the land flattened, a farmstead. But the sparseness of settlements northwest of Oslo was a vivid reminder that Norway is a nation of 5.5 million people in a vast northern landscape of 125,000 square miles (324,000 square km).

We were headed towards Flåm, a tiny village of a few hundred people at the southernmost finger tip of Aurlandsfjord, which itself is at the end of Norway's longest fjord, Sogenfjorden. This would be our introduction to fjord country. The land gradually rose before us, hills tending towards mountain humps as we headed west. Then, without warning, we went into a tunnel that seemed never-ending. It went on five kilometers, ten, fifteen, twenty! It was, in fact *24.5 kilometers long.* Only later did we realize this was the famous Lærdal Tunnel, the longest tunnel in the world.

The tunnel finally spat us back into daylight at the village of Aurland, near the edge of the water. After so long in the dark, our heads nearly exploded with the spectacular view. The vast fjord stretched out before us in full sunlight. Massive cliffs towered nine hundred meters, plunging almost vertically into deep blue waters right by the roadside. Even in mid-June the mountaintops above the cliffs were still white with snow. We felt dizzy and disoriented just looking out across the water at so much verticality.

Our Airbnb was just up the valley in a little hamlet where the Flåm River meets the end of the fjord. The harbor consisted of ferry docks, a train station and railyard, several hotels, three restaurants, a grocery store and a bunch of tourist shops. The villagers' houses were a bit upstream, on the flat land along the sides of the rushing, aquamarine river.

Next morning we were up early for a ferry ride from Aurlandsfjord to Nærøyfjord which, Teresa informed me casually, both happen to be UNESCO World Heritage Sites. The world's leading cultural-scientific body agrees these are the most crazy-ass-awesome fjords in the world. The ferry was an uber-cool all electric, hydro-powered ferry, one of several next-gen, emission-free ferries that ply these still waters.

The ferry silently glided north up Aurlandsfjord, then did a U-turn south, down the adjoining Nærøyfjord ("narrow-fjord"), a long, narrow fjord rimmed by some of the highest cliffs in Norway. They not only rise up 900 meters, below the water the rock walls plunge as much as 1,300 meters down. We had wondered why we did not see any sailboats anchored along the way. Answer: the water is simply too deep for any anchor to find bottom.

Nærøyfjord's most captivating feature was the myriad waterfalls cascading down its sides. White ribbons and braids leapt from the clifftops, some with such force that when they landed on a rock, they spouted upwards, creating dramatic plumes of spray. In any national park elsewhere in the world, a single one of these falls would be a major attraction. Here there were falls wherever you turned your head. There was just so much water... where did it all come from?

I got a second close look at Nærøyfjord a few days later, when I signed on for a half-day kayaking tour that started in the town of Gudvangen, at the very end of the fjord. Here, the cliffs seem to circle the town like the walls of a vast natural cathedral, and the waterfalls streaming down all sides look as if they are descending from the heavens. This might account for the Norse meaning of *Gudvangen*: "The Place of the Gods."

There was a Viking settlement here more than a thousand years ago. There's little of it left, though, as most Viking settlements were made of wood, which decays. That makes it hard to tell whether or not Gudvangen was a place of ceremony and ritual, except for the name. Nevertheless, some enterprising Norwegian took the opportunity to build a modern-day Viking village here, complete with in-costume residents and tour guides. Since I arrived early for my paddle, I bought a ticket and joined the Viking tour. Our host, in regulation leather jerkin, demonstrated several techniques for dismembering and decapitating foes with an axe and with a sword. He explained that a good sword took over a year to make and cost six horses. Axes were cheaper, and often a Viking's weapon of choice, as it was so much more versatile.

I could not linger to try my hand at axe throwing or rune casting because it was time to paddle. I was soon in a wetsuit, splashing along with six other kayakers. Kayaking has been my source of connection with the wilderness for the past fifteen years. I owned two boats back in Bethesda, Maryland, and used to go out on a wild stretch of the Potomac River a couple of times a week. Since departing for Europe seven months ago, I've not had one chance to paddle, until now.

Entranced by the waterfalls, the vibrant greenness of the lower slopes, the crest of snow on the mountains above, I thought of the Vikings who lived in these waters, and named

Left: A Viking-era longboat at Gudvangen. Right: my kayak, 1,000 years later.

this spot the Place of the Gods. I suppose that was their way of declaring the fjord a UNESCO World Heritage Site.

Maui, our 21-year-old Māori New Zealander kayking guide was cool, devilishly handsome, and completely relaxed. This was his first summer guiding in Norway. He said he hated the cold, and left home to avoid the New Zealand winter. Ruefully, he told me he did not realize he would be spending every weekend guiding kayakers along the fjord, making camp, and then next morning trekking up a winding twelve-mile trail to the *snowfields* at the top of the cliffs.

These snowfields, I soon learned, are the source of all that cascading water, and also the key to understanding the forces that formed the fjords. This part of Norway is just barely south of Iceland, basically on the same latitude as Alaska. So, even though it was T-shirt weather at the bottom of the fjords, at the top it was still freezing cold. Norway had many Ice Ages in the last 2.6 million years, and they lasted longer than in the rest of Europe. Before the big chills, most of central Norway was a great rocky plateau, like a giant pancake. The western edge of it formed a smooth unbroken coastline along the Atlantic. No fjords.

Of course, everybody knows the fjords are the product of erosion due to glaciers, but it never occurred to me how powerful a force that erosion must have been to gouge out hundreds of long and deep furrows from that massive plateau. I found a great website that explained the geological forces at work, the aptly-named *www.fjords.com*. Fortuitously, the site focused on the formation of Sognefjord:

> From the original (paleic) landscape, at that time only penetrated by a single river system, the glaciers abrased, plucked, gnawed and washed away an amount of rock corresponding to roughly 7,600 cubic kilometers, resulting in a valley 204000 meters long and a maximum relief of 2850 meters.

Let's imagine 7,600 cubic kilometers in concrete terms:

Picture one cubic kilometer—a kilometer high, a kilometer long, a kilometer wide. If you had a box that size, you could fit 400 Great Pyramids of Giza inside it. Now, stack a thousand of these 1 km x 1 km boxes in a row. It would stretch out 1,000 km/600 miles, roughly the distance from Washington D.C. to Chicago. Finally, stack that wall 7.6 km high. That's approximately seven-and-a-half boxes (about 5 miles high, something in between Mount McKinley and Mount Everest). That's how much rock was pushed out by the glaciers just to make Sognefjord.

So, how did that erosion actually happen? It surprised me to learn it happened *fast*. Recall the limestone cliffs of the Algarve in Portugal or the Dolomite mountains of Italy were shaped over a few hundred million years. Norway's fjords, in contrast, were formed in just 2.6 million years—one percent of the time that it took nature to create the Dolomites! A veritable blink of the eye, in geological time.

During that period there were 40 Ice Ages in Europe. In each glaciation the ice in western Norway piled up to three kilometers thick. The glaciers flowed outwards slowly, like a thick, icy syrup poured from heaven on the center of the pancake. Under tremendous pressure, these growing glaciers picked up gravel and loose stones that got embedded in the bottom of the ice, turning the glaciers into giant sanders that scraped over the plateau, wearing deep grooves in the landscape.

With each successive Ice Age these grooves gouged deeper, eventually forming valleys over two kilometers from top to bottom, and dozens of kilometers long. Glacial valleys have a characteristic "U" shape: steep at the sides, sloped at the bottom, where sediment left over from the grinding settles. If the valley floor is above water, the sediment turns into soil and life takes root. When glaciers grow into the ocean and then retreat, they fill with water, forming fjords. Beyond the geological science of it, what leaves me amazed is how artistically Norway's giant pancake has been carved into fingers of fjords, each one a distinct expression of the power of ice over stone.

As I complete this story of the fjords, I look across the water at a confluence of valleys that flow from Jostedal Glacier into Nordfjord. Jostedal is the largest remaining glacier in continental Europe. The ice above glints in the late evening sunshine. The glacier feels much like a living entity. Perhaps it will bide its time for several thousand years in these high northern mountains until human-caused climate changed has passed. Then, when the earth finally turns cold again, it will flow down these green valleys, once more sculpting the rock into new, incredibly beautiful forms.

Chapter 31

Highway to Hjelle

The little village of Hjelle is tucked right at the backside of Lake Strynevatnet, about five hours' drive northwest of Oslo in fjord country. There's nothing more than a cluster of wooden houses in a sheltered cove and the quaint Hjelle Hotel by the water's edge.

The hotel was built in 1896 as part of Norway's first tourist boom. Norway, in fact, claims to have invented scenic tourism, right here in the fjords. Europe's upper classes, particularly the English, had discovered the fjords in the latter part of the 1800s and found them pleasing. Steamers full of sightseers began showing up in remote farming and fishing villages. Hotels like the one at Hjelle started popping up. But they had little to offer the visitors aside from the stupendous views. To entice them to stay longer and spend their money, Norwegians started building scenic roads through the mountains to give the rich

The author's photo of a Norwegian National Trust poster at Hjelle.

155

sight-seers the opportunity to go for a drive and explore. But, go for a drive *in what*? Enterprising hotel owners brought in high-end, new-fangled automobiles for hire, like these, below:

Hjelle got into the action. The village decided to build a road all the way up the valley to where it intersected another new scenic highway that connected Oslo to the fjord village of Geiranger, which was also experiencing a tourist boom. The highway to Hjelle began in 1884 and took 12 years to build, with crews working from both ends toward the middle. Pictures of the road-workers look grim. The workers had to carry large guardstones (as shown in the photo above) up the road on their backs.

Happily, the road has been improved in the past century, but is still open only in summer; there's too much snow the rest of the year. Until 1950, the route had to be shoveled clear every spring, *by hand*. It could take the road crews up to two months, as the snow piled as much as 13 meters (40 feet) deep in places.

However, the weather was warm and sunny this first of July when we left Hjelle. The old scenic road wound up a steep gorge that gradually levelled out into a high-altitude, U-shaped glacial valley. Ahead of us, the sides of the valley were mottled with patches of snow which grew thicker and deeper as we climbed. Suddenly, there was snow everywhere, and we came upon an operating ski lift. We pulled in for a hot chocolate at the café at the base of the lift, and marveled at the white slope, filled with skiers and snowboarders. The sign read "Summer Skiing." I've never before seen a ski slope that only operates in summertime.

Beyond the ski run, the road kept rising. We drove across a surreal landscape—a vast field of boulders, dropped on the valley floor by melting glaciers from the last Ice Age. We stopped for lunch by the roadside with not a building in sight. All we had to eat in the car was salt and vinegar potato chips, a bag of cherries, and a half bottle of *vinho verde*. Not much of

Lunch is served!

a menu, but flâneurs adapt. Seated on a couple of rocks in the
sunshine, surrounded by snow and the chocolate-brown rubble
hills, this was one of the most memorable meals of our trip.

Over the high alpine pass, the highway from Hjelle joined
the road to Geiranger on the top of the great, high mass of the
Norwegian plateau. Here the road leveled out, and we settled in
for a what we thought would be a humdrum drive. But the road
kept climbing, and soon took us through an even higher snow-
filled valley, flanked by a massive black massif and a frozen
lake. A glacier, visible at the top of the massif, scraped against
the clouds.

Teresa spotted a sign indicating a side road to the Dalsnibba.
Oh, we have to take that road! She was adamant. Her guidebook
said it was the best viewpoint in the whole Geiranger area. Now,
I won't say that I grumbled about having seen enough views for
a single day, not even when we stopped at a toll booth and paid
$15 to proceed. But I thought to myself, *this had better be good.*

After a day of precipitous driving, you would think we would get used to the hairpin turn roads with cliffs for edges. But this switchback trail up to Dalsnibba took "scary" to a whole new level. Teresa, in the passenger seat, chanted a mantra over and over again as I swerved up toward the sky:

"Ohmygodohmygodohfuckmefuckmeicantlookimgonnadie!"

Eventually, we got to the rocky outcropping that formed the top of Dalsnibba, and I realized exactly why Teresa made us drive here. The viewpoint, in fact, hung over the cliff edge. We could look straight down 500 meters through the iron grating at our feet. The road wriggled far beneath us. Beyond, the valley opened out to Geiranger and the still, green waters of the fjord. In the photo, below, you can see a large white oval in the water that looks like a grain of rice—that's a cruise ship docked at

The view of Geiranger from Dalsnibba. Can you spot the cruise ship?

Geiranger. It's carrying as many as 3,000 passengers who have come from all over the world to gaze at Norway's fjords.

I later learned that in the summer months this tiny village receives an average of 6,000 visitors per day. Dozens upon dozens of buses and bike rentals shuttle them up to various viewpoints or onto the hiking trails. There's a modern fjord center, which explains the history and geology of the region, art galleries, restaurants, and boat rentals.

Norway has done well, as the world comes to see its splendors. Indeed, *National Geographic Traveller Magazine* declared these fjords the worldwide best scenic destination of all UNESCO Natural World Heritage Sites. What I particularly appreciate is the nation's commitment to balancing developing of the tourism industry with maintaining the natural beauty of the fjords, including electric motors on many of the tour boats and vehicles.

This was even true at the Geiranger Grande Fjord Hotel, where we arrived at the end of our long day. Teresa hit the mattress, announcing she would remain thus ensconced until dinner. We were both utterly exhausted from five hours of sheer exhilaration on the road. When at last we were ready to head into town for a meal, the hotel offered us a complimentary shuttle ride in their chartreuse-green Porsche.

That's right, the hotel keeps up the tradition of those early Norwegian tour operators of the late 1800s, offering high-end car rentals for a day, or even just a few speedy hours. Our driver explained, as he accelerated along the curvy, narrow road, that the car is also an electric vehicle: a *green*, green Porsche.

Chapter 32

A Tale of Peril in Geirangerfjord

The massive car ferry passed our tiny, ten-foot boat in the middle of the fjord. The ship was about two hundred and fifty feet long, maybe sixty feet wide, and left a wave in its wake about three feet high. I'd managed waves almost this big in Geirangerfjord just the previous day in a kayak. Now Teresa and I were alone in a small, open-topped motorboat. The fjord is usually so calm, local boathouses rent boats like this one to tourists just on their say-so that they know what they are doing. The attendant had

Left: Teresa at the bow. Right: The ferry in the photo is about half the size of the one we encountered in the fjord. The white speck in the water directly above the bow of the ferry is a motorboat the size of ours.

simply thrown us each a life preserver and pushed the little boat away from the dock.

I was at the throttle in the rear, while Teresa sat at the bow as we zoomed along the fjord. I was pretty confident we could handle the situation with the looming ferry, even if I had not steered a motorboat in, well, decades.

But I have kayaked for the past 18 years, and I know that small craft can get swamped or even capsize in a situation like this is if the wake of the ship hits from the side. To prevent this in a kayak, you aim straight for the oncoming wave at 90 degrees, and paddle fast. The momentum keeps you upright and moving as you bob up and down. You get a little wet, but don't tip. No problem. It's easier in a motorboat, I figured, because the bow is higher above the water than in a kayak, and you go can go faster.

When she saw the ferry steaming in our direction, Teresa, urged me to get close to the shore, a note of panic in her voice. But that's a bad strategy in a fjord like this one. The shore is a sheer rock wall, and the waves would bounce right back at us — amplified, as the incoming and reflecting waves cross paths (a lesson I learned the hard way from that beach walk around the cliffs in the Algarve).

So, I held course for the ship's wake and kicked up the throttle. *No worries, sweetheart!* We had already weathered the wakes of two smaller ships, so I was not scared. But I knew the sheer depth of the fjord kind of freaked out my beloved. The rock walls surrounding us were a kilometer up, and the green water beneath us was hundreds of meters deep. We had talked about how the massive scale of it all made us feel tiny and vulnerable.

We hit the ship's wake. The bow of our boat shot up, then tipped down fast into the trough behind it. Quick physics question: If a wave is three feet high, how deep is the trough behind it? Right! Another three feet. Quick math question, three plus three equals what? Right again! A six-foot drop. Our bow slammed into the bottom of the trough hard and popped up again onto the next wave like a rollercoaster. Like a rollercoaster with no safety bar, no seatbelt, and nothing to grab on to.

As we crested that second wave, the boat pivoted vertically like a see-saw, exactly like you get at the top of a rollercoaster. From the back of the boat, I saw Teresa, directly ahead of me and facing forward, slowly lift off her seat and roll backwards. What an optical illusion! In fact, she only appeared to be moving. In reality, she was staying relatively still, obedient to the laws of inertia while the boat was rolling forward over the wave. I was fascinated.

From my perspective, as the bow dropped and the stern lifted, Teresa seemed to float in space and spin ever so slowly backwards. As she performed this graceful, space-ballet maneuver, she stuck both her legs out directly in front of her in a "V" formation as if riding an upside down invisible horse. The back of the boat rose up to meet her as she completed her dismount, bottoms up, landing surprisingly gently with the back of her head and shoulders resting on my feet.

Her first words to me after this truly remarkable aerobatic routine were: "I can't believe you are laughing at me!"

We were through the worst of the waves, and I could barely hold it together, I was laughing so hard.

"From now on, I have to wear one of those helmet cameras," I said, when I could speak again. "So I can capture your spontaneous acrobatics for posterity."

"I almost *died*!" she exclaimed, furiously, "and you are *laughing*? I was airborne! I could have gone over! I was flying, and I didn't know where I was going to come down! I literally blacked out for a few seconds. I had no idea what was happening. I could have gone over! And then you would have had to go in after me, so it would not have been a great day for *you* either!"

In retrospect, I realize I had neglected a key difference between kayaks and motorboats. You are locked in place in a kayak cockpit. You move with the boat. Not so with a our little shell. Teresa did not even have a handle to hold on to. Also, her sitting at the front put extra weight on the bow which caused it to drop harder into the trough. Had I known, I would have asked her to move to the back of the boat with me as we approached the waves—I belatedly found all that wonderful advice online.

"I could have died," my beloved grumbled once more, resettling herself on the front seat, smoothing the last of her ruffled feathers.

What is truly remarkable about Teresa is that she does not stay in a bad mood for long. After a few minutes, we were back to enjoying the ride, and the magnificent views of Geirangerfjord, all the way home.

***

There is one actual tale of peril I'd like to share about enchanting Geiranger: the village, and several others on the shores of the fjord, will inevitably be destroyed by a massive tsunami. A crack is widening on Åknesfjället, one of the mountains on the sides of the fjord. It runs 700 meters long, and in places 30 meters wide. Sooner or later, the whole mountainside will slide into the fjord: 150 million tons of rock. Experts predict a tsunami wave up to 80 meters high will follow.

When will it happen? 30 years from now or 100? No one knows. Teams of geologists monitor the crack round the clock. They say they will be able to give people a 72-hours warning before the collapse. Because of this, residents say—to the tourists at least—that they live in the safest fjord in Norway. But the school runs regular evacuation drills for the children. Life in the fjord is perilous. And not just when you are out for a ride in all that vastness on a tiny boat.

Chapter 33

Trolls and Trollstigen

Today we headed for *Trollstigen*. "The Troll Stairs" is one of Norway's most tortuous mountain passes in a country famous for its dizzying drives. Trollstigen drops 858 meters in 11 hairpin turns down a steep stone slope on the side of a mountain, bracketed by torrential waterfalls on either side. The overall effect is of giant steps carved in the rock. Hence the evocative name.

Trolls hold a special place in Norway's culture and mythology. While some are small (the kind we are familiar with in North America as the little plastic "troll dolls" with bright-colored tufts of hair), some are human sized (as featured in Ibsen's famous opera, *Peer Gynt*) the *real* trolls—the ones of old Norse legends—are massive creatures who dwell in the most remote and desolate landscapes: Forest Trolls, Mountain Trolls, Ice Trolls. Some are so large they are often mistaken for mountains themselves as they slumber, and woe to the hapless human who awakens one!

Twelve years ago, a satirical Norwegian movie called *Troll Hunter* appeared, which was hilarious precisely because of the ubiquity of the troll legends. It was a mocumentary about three college students following around a troll hunter, who worked for the Norwegian Department of Trolls. His job was to rein in rogue trolls and to cover up their damage with false stories of windstorms and tornados, so the willfully-deceived Norwegian people never had to face the reality of trolls in their midst. One of the best jokes was that power lines through the wilderness were actually electric fences for containing trolls.

Norwegians seem to delight in their troll mythology. There's a troll park on the Island of Senja, complete with a life-sized model of a seated troll the size of a house. And there's a troll museum in Tromsø, with a faux scientific typology of the different kinds of trolls and their habits, plus histories, legends, and a guide for troll spotting.

Teresa and I thought we saw a troll while we were boating the previous week in Geirangerfjord. We passed a cliff that held a massive chiseled face in the rock, with a green goatee on its chin. In these vast landscapes, if you go looking for trolls, you will certainly find them!

As we drove towards *Trollstigen*, we mused about what might have impelled early Norwegians to have imagined trolls

Troll spotting in Geirangerfjord.

Mountain troll country

in the first place. Since arriving at the fjords, we both sensed this land is different from anything else we have experienced. Yes, the Alps have vast grandeur, the Dolomites have awe-inspiring pinnacles. But there's something about the fjords and mountains of Norway that makes us feel both awed and little bit scared as we flâmotor through them.

"It feels something like vertigo," I said to Teresa while driving, "My eyes can't process the size of what I'm looking at. I can't fit the fjords, the cliffs, the peaks together into a single perceptual framework. It's dizzying, like a fear of falling, but falling up, falling out: out into something so big it threatens to dissolve us."

Teresa replied that she thought this peculiar sensation has something to do with Norway's waterfalls: "We're used to mountains that are still, like in a painting," she mused, "maybe with one waterfall added in. But in Norway there's falling water everywhere. That makes it seem as if the mountains are moving, too. Alive, in a way that feels ominous. A presence. The noise of the water fills the air. It speaks, it growls. So it's easy to imagine why people believed that trolls lived here."

Abruptly a sign appeared on the side of the road, marking the path to the lookout above Trollstigen. We parked. The mists moved in and out, causing the mountains above to loom into existence and then vanish completely as we walked along the wet trail. We followed the path of the river to where it plunged over the abyss, and then on to the lookout point, which hung over the edge between the two falls. From there, looking straight down, Trollstigen faded into cloud and then reemerged. It was disorienting. The whole landscape seemed to be in motion, shifting orientation with the mist.

Even more discombobulating, on our way back to the car, we stepped into the tourist gift shop, which sported rows and rows of tiny, kitschy, souvenir troll dolls. Come on! These are not the fearsome beings that slumber in these ominous hills. I felt appalled and disenchanted. I guess it is a natural human impulse, to turn something fearful into something cute and harmless... like a teddy bear. Are we doing it just for the children — or to convince ourselves that we're safe?

Luckily, before shaking off the rain and getting back in the car, I found something that restored my sense of awe. One of the informational plaques by the visitors' center described a Stone Age archeological find near Trollstigen. It was a U-shaped wall made of piled rocks that prehistoric hunters built to hide behind when stalking reindeer. What was unusual is that this wall was built high up on the mountainside, not in the valley, where, logically, they could more easily have hunted. According to archeologists, this indicates the wall might well have been erected when glaciers still filled the surrounding valleys — meaning people were living *here*, on the edge of Trollstigen, during the last Ice Age, more that 13,000 years ago, and quite possibly earlier.

I wonder, did these Stone Age reindeer hunters, the first who made this wild, vast space their home, sense the presence of trolls? Are they the ones who created the first myths, and passed them down to Norway's neolithic peoples, and thence to the Vikings, medieval Christians, and finally the modern makers of monster movies and kitschy troll dolls?

To our surprise, driving down Trollstigen in mist and rain was actually not so scary compared to other mountain switchbacks we have driven in Norway. Teresa and I wondered if descending through clouds actually made it less nerve-wracking. Because, cloaked in fog, we could not see the trolls.

Chapter 34

The Most Beautiful Town in Norway

The town of Ålesund (pronounced "Oh-le-sund") was voted the most beautiful town in Norway in a recent survey of Norwegians.

"Why," you ask, incredulous, "would a little cod-fishing town on a remote island, tucked between the wild north Atlantic and a rugged mountainous plateau, deserve such an honor?"

Because Ålesund has the largest concentration of Art Nouveau buildings *in the entire world*. Several hundred of these century-old houses are all clustered together on this little island. A walk around the town center leaves you breathless from the gorgeousness of so much whimsy embedded in such a wild, gray, and rainy landscape. The town is simply stunning to behold, the houses painted vivid pinks, yellows and greens, soft mauve or sky blue. Around every corner there's a turret or a spire, a floral bas-relief or even a face embedded in the walls.

"But hang on," I hear a note of surprise in your voice, "Isn't Budapest famous for Art Nouveau? What about Vienna? Paris? How the heck could this tiny town, nothing but a speck on a map of the coast of Norway, end up with block after block of what today are considered the architectural treasures of central Europe?"

What an astute question!

The answer is simple, tragic, inspiring, and lucky.

A fire destroyed 80% of Ålesund in January 1904, leaving more than 10,000 people homeless in the middle of winter. Amazingly, only one person died in the flames. Nearby communities sent emergency aid at once, and within a few days four German relief ships arrived, filled with food, medical supplies, and

Ålesund, Art Nouveau capital of Norway.

everything needed to build emergency shelters—a gift from Kaiser Wilhelm, who often vacationed in the impressive fjords nearby, and knew Ålesund well.

Norwegian architects, including those who were educated and employed abroad—in England, Germany, Austria— dropped what they were doing and came to Ålesund. They brought with them the latest trend in architecture and design: *Art Noveau*. This new, expressive style drew inspiration from forms found in nature, with curves and flourishes, vines and flowers. Meanwhile, Norwegian construction workers and tradesmen soon arrived *en masse* from all over the country. A national depression had left many of them unemployed, so when news of the fire and subsequent rebuilding effort spread, they simply headed to Ålesund, where every skilled hand was put to work.

One final stroke of luck: just a few short years before the fire, home insurance companies began operating in the region. As a result, most of Ålesund's houses were insured when the fire struck.

The reconstruction of Ålesund coincided with the independence of Norway, after 400 years of rule by Denmark and Sweden. This lent a sense of patriotic pride to the project, a desire to show the world what Norway was capable of. That sense of nationalism led the architects to infuse distinctly Norwegian elements into the design of their buildings, borrowing Viking-era motifs known as *Dragestil*, or "Dragon Style," like these, below:

Teresa and I took an Art-Nouveau guided tour through town with a lovely local resident named Randi, her graying blonde hair held in a single, thick braid. Randi was born and raised in

Dragestil **flourishes on Ålesund's Art Nouveau façades.**

Ålesund in the '60s and '70s, and she told us that when she was young, she thought the town was so boring, so drab!

"That's because all these houses," she gestured towards the brightly colored streets, "were never painted! The beautiful colors we see in Ålesund today weren't there for the first 70 years after the fire. After the architects and builders were finished, they left town. By then, the insurance money had run out. So the residents and shop owners simply never got around to painting their new homes and businesses!"

By the 1970s, Randi told us, people were starting to tear down their now old Art Nouveau houses and replace them with more modern homes.

"What saved them?" you ask, your relentless curiosity still undimmed.

This was also our question to Randi. By way of an answer, she led us to a larger-than-life statue of an old man next to the bridge in the center of town.

"This is Harald Grytten," she introduced us to the statue as if to an old friend. "He single-handedly convinced the citizens of Ålesund not to tear down its Art Nouveau houses, and instead, to paint them as originally intended. He lives in Ålesund to this day... he's quite a character!"

Grytten is portrayed in this sculpture as a rather glum, craggy-featured old man. His hand makes an open, palm-out gesture, as if to say, "Isn't it obvious what we must do? This is our heritage. We must preserve these houses for the good of our town!"

Today, this heritage has put Ålesund on the map as something utterly unique, and one of the most visited tourist destinations in Norway.

"What an amazing man! What an amazing tale of a town!" I hear you exclaim, satisfied, at last, now that all your questions about Ålesund have been answered.

Chapter 35

Polestar 2 the Arctic

Teresa and I have been zooming around Norway for a month now in our white Polestar 2 electric vehicle. At last we have reached Trondheim, the final city on our path to the Arctic.

Norway is shaped kind of like a drooping mandolin or sitar, with a round bulbous body in the south, a long thin neck that runs up between the coastline and the Swedish border, and then an oblong head at the top, above the Arctic Circle. Trondheim is situated right where the neck begins stretching north. From this staging point, we will begin our long drive to Norkapp, the northern-most point of mainland Europe.

It's as far north as Barrow on the north coast of Alaska. The drive is about 1,600 km — roughly 1,000 miles — from Trondheim. We plan on taking our time, exploring the wild terrain along the way. But, there are bound to be fewer chargers along the route, and probably fewer emergency vehicles if one happens to run out of juice on a remote northern road.

Overall, we've managed okay with our Polestar 2 this first month. I think I've experienced most of the things that can go wrong. True, some charging stations have defeated me and I've had to move along. Sometimes the charging apps don't work, or the station is out of order. Once, my charging cable got stuck and I couldn't unplug it. Two company technicians had to come out and wrangle it loose. But we've never come close to running out of juice. Other than *range anxiety*, the car's been a dream to drive: great pick up, great steering, and the onboard navigator helps you find nearby charging stations. I remain optimistic.

Just when I was feeling like a modern-day Arctic explorer, I was introduced to Børge Ousland, a *real* Norwegian explorer.

Ousland is a household name in Norway for his several daring expeditions to both North and South Poles. Just few years ago he and a fellow explorer, Mike Horn, made international headlines for completing an expedition to the North Pole, on skis, in the middle of winter. Each man pulled 400 kg of gear on sleds over the ice. It took them three months, traveling in complete darkness much of the time, in temperatures as low as minus 50 degrees Celsius.

He's in his late fifties, about five years younger than I am. Did I mention my epic struggle with range anxiety? My heroic battle with the stuck charging cable? Well, I suppose we each find our own edge in our adventures. There will always be someone more daring, and frankly, I think Teresa is happy that mastering an EV in the Arctic is the upper limit of my sexagenarian thrill-seeking.

Trondheim is a place to catch our breath and gather our wits, before heading up Norway's neck on our own expedition.

It's a disorientingly typical European city compared to the other places we have visited in Norway. The mountain fjords and rocky islands require adaptation to the land and the climate: houses perch on the hills or cling to the shoreline; they are built to shelter from avalanches or withstand gales. But Trondheim has a surprisingly mild climate. It's surrounded by gently rolling, fertile hills and valleys that easily could be mistaken for rural Virginia. The region is one of the two main farming areas in Norway (the other is just north of Oslo), in a country where only *three percent* of the land is suitable for agriculture. The rest is forest, mountian, and ice. We know the land to the north of us will be rougher, colder, and wetter.

In Trondheim we met up a second time with our Norwegian friend from Oslo, Roald. He too is on his way up the neck. He's visiting his sister in the far nothern village where he was born and raised. In summertime, many Norwegians return to their birthplace in remote regions. It's a salmon-like impulse, I suppose. Happily, Roald was traveling upstream along the E6 National Highway at the same time as us. So, we not only crossed paths in Trondheim, he also invited us to stop by for a visit to his home town further along our route.

Roald arrived at our hotel in a light shirt, khakis and sandals—no socks—and he happily sat out on the terrace bar while we were bundled in sweaters. "Oh, I don't get cold," he told us.

Roald told us Trondheim was founded in 997 A.D. as Norway's first capital by King Olaf. Olaf had been a brutal Viking leader, but a near death experience led him to convert to Christianity. He became the first Christian Viking king, and he made it his mission to convert his people from their pagan ways. For those who resisted, his methods of persuasion included torture and execution. This did not make him popular. Olaf was eventually killed during a battle against his pagan brethren. After his death, this violent king became Saint Olaf. Trondheim's Cathedral has supposedly enshrined his remains. His successors, also entombed in the cathedral, completed Olaf's mission and Christianized Norway.

As we wished each other safe journey on the road, Roald gave us one parting word of advice: "Always remember, there is no shame in turning back."

We laughed. Turn back? No way. We may not be pulling sleds to the North Pole, but we are riding our Polestar 2 all the way to the top of Europe.

Chapter 36

Crossing the Arctic Circle

Today, Teresa and I crossed the Arctic Circle.

Norway's E6 highway intersects this imaginary, dotted line on the globe at a barren, mountain pass. Snow-streaked hills rim the horizon. It's cold, windswept, vast. In 1989 Norway declared the surrounding 2,770 square kilometers a national park, as an area that has remained "untouched by the mark of modern times."

Where the highway crosses the Circle, there's a massive visitors' center. You can't miss it. It's the only building in sight as far as the eye can see. The center sells all sorts of Arctic-Circle swag for tourists, including T-shirts that announce, "I Crossed the Arctic Circle." There's even an Arctic Circle certificate one can buy, somehow making it official. The center features a stuffed moose, a frighteningly massive polar bear, and other dead animals. Plus the obligatory troll-doll tableau.

Next to the center there's a wooden monument, gray and weathered by the elements. It's ringed by the coats of arms of Norway's few-dozen northern community districts. The wood is etched all over with copies of rock carvings from the early peoples of the far north. Their descendants, the Sámi, still live in the Arctic, and this monument seems to declare that they own this place just as much as does the modern state.

Past the monument and up a small hill is a field filled with little rock cairns that visitors have built to mark their presence. Teresa and I each added a stone to one of them. The urge was irresistible: *We made it here!*

As we were savoring the moment, a most *un*savory question arose in my mind: Why is the Arctic Circle always *dotted* on the map? Is it just some arbitrary pencil marks on the globe that delineates what some elite cabal of geographers and cartographers considered "Arctic"? What makes this imaginary line worth all the fuss? *Wikipedia*, as ever, came quickly to my rescue:

> The Arctic Circle marks the southernmost latitude at which, on the December solstice, the shortest day of the year in the northern hemisphere, the sun will not rise all day, and on the June solstice, the longest day of the year in the northern hemisphere, the sun will not set. These phenomena are referred to as polar night and midnight sun respectively, and the further north one progresses, the more pronounced these effects become.

Simply put, above the Arctic Circle, for at least one day a year, the sun does not set. Dang, how did I not know this? I checked my weather app. Indeed, for the first time in our trip through Norway, there would be no sunset where we were going to sleep that night, in Narvik. In fact, we are going far enough north that we won't see a sunset for another three weeks.

What I found most cool is that the Arctic Circle actually *moves* from year to year. It is not, actually a permanent line on the map, like, for instance, the Equator. Back to *Wikipedia*:

> The position of the Arctic Circle is not fixed and currently runs 66°33′49.1″ north of the Equator. Its latitude depends on the Earth's axial tilt, which fluctuates within a margin of more than 2° over a 41,000-year period, owing to tidal forces resulting from the orbit of the Moon. Consequently, the Arctic Circle is currently *drifting northwards at a speed of about 14.5 m (48 ft) per year* [italics mine].

Whoah! Wait a minute! The Arctic Circle Center website says it was built in 1990, and that the Circle runs right through its middle. If that were true in 1990, 32 years ago, then: 48 feet/ year x 32 years = 1,536 feet. That's a bit more than a quarter of a mile the Arctic Circle has shifted. So the center is now that far *south* of the actual imaginary dotted line that marks the Circle, and so are all those little cairns and names written in stone. All those tourist selfies at the monument actually don't show them at the Circle at all. It's like getting your picture taken in Paris at the street next to the Eiffel Tower, or in Niagara at a bar a few blocks away from the Falls.

I wish the T-shirts they sold at the center announced: "I missed the Arctic Circle by a quarter of a mile." That, certainly, is what mine would have to say.

A couple of mature flâneurs get their picture taken just south of the Arctic Circle.

Chapter 37

The Man from Dangerous River

Roald Skøelv's surname comes from the river that runs next to the house where he was born. *Skø* means "dangerous," and *elv* means "waters," but is often applied to rivers. Skøelv—the River Skø—flows into the fjord just a stone's thrown from Roald's family farmhouse, here in Norway's western Arctic.

Teresa and I first met Roald in Washington D.C. in the year 2000. He was the manager of a media training program we delivered several times a year for the International Monetary Fund (IMF). Roald was a big bear of a man, tall and broad shouldered. It was easier to imagine him as a Viking, rowing across the Atlantic, than supervising communications workshops for economists.

Roald turned out to be one of the most affable and easy-going professionals we ever worked with. He was one of those rare individuals who somehow managed to be his authentic self on the job. He really cared about the people he worked with; he wanted the best for them—it was never about his next promotion. After he left the IMF for a position at the World Bank, we kept in touch, met for lunch from time to time, and became good friends. Eventually, he and his wife returned to Norway and retired.

When Roald learned we were driving to the Arctic, he invited us to visit him in Skøelv, where he returns every summer. He promised to show us not only his family farmhouse, but the whole remote area where he grew up. We were able to book two nights at an Airbnb in a village just ten minutes from Skøelv.

When we arrived at the cluster of homes where the River Skøelv meets the fjord, Roald greeted us and took us home to meet his sister, Toril, in the old family farmhouse. Toril lives just outside of Oslo most of the year, but she also returns to Skøelv every summer. Her daughter now works in the village as a teacher, and so Toril has grandaughters here, too. She stays for the whole season, keeps the farmhouse maintained, and fills the deck with a profusion of beautiful flowers.

The house sits right at the edge of the beach, giving them a sweeping view of the strait, and the island of Senja beyond. There are two mountains on the other side of the road, which means there was little land to cultivate—just enough sloping hillside to feed several sheep and a few cows. Roald told us one of the mountains was called "Dinner Mountain," because when the sun was on top of it, that meant it was time to come home for dinner.

We sat out on the deck and drank coffee while Roald and Toril told us stories of growing up in this old wooden house, built by their great-grandfather who came here from Senja over 100 years ago. He built the first house in Skøelv and established the first farm. At that time, the government was encouraging people to forego the tradition of taking their father's name as their surname (as in, Leif Erickson), and instead to choose a family name that could be passed on through generations, as was the practice in most other European nations. So, when Great-grandfather moved here, he took the name of the river as his new surname. The small community of Skøelv bloomed around him. Still today, many of Roald and Toril's relatives live within walking distance from their farm, and most of them are named Skøelv.

Roald remembers working the farm as a boy: leading sheep up the hillside to pasture, cutting fodder on the steep hillsides with a hand-scythe with his father, and the annual walk he made with the cow, upriver to the farm that owned the only bull in the village. The farmers and their wives along the road would always tease the boy about what was about to happen! He also remembers the beach, literally right outside his door, where he and his friends would play and swim during the long summer days.

Most vividly, though, Roald remembers the moment in his childhood when he realized he would have to decide whether to stay in the village and learn to integrate into this small world, or *get out*. Toril, for example, left when she turned eighteen and got a job in Oslo as a telephone operator.

For Roald, education became his route to the world beyond the farm. He scored top marks in middle school, and convinced his parents to send him to high school—the first in his family to get so much education. He then studied languages at the University of Trondheim, and went on to graduate school in Chicago. Seven years after he left Skøelv, he returned to Norway's north coast (with a wife and small child) for a teaching job in a tiny town much like the one where he grew up.

I'm still not sure exactly how Roald ended up in Washington D.C. with his second wife. But if there is one thing the arc of his life demonstrates to me, it's that no matter how far across the ocean a salmon may swim, it will still find its way back to the fjord where it was spawned.

It's not just Roald and his sister. Many Norwegians who migrated south to the cities when young find themselves going back to remote areas for holiday as adults. Whether ancestral homes or modern cabins, there seems to be a national longing for connection to the wilderness. A half-million Norwegians, literally one-in-ten people, own a cabin or cottage. Which means virtually everyone in the country has access to one.

I did make one *faux-pas* at dinner that evening. Toril served us a hearty, homemade meat-and-pasta soup, which I couldn't eat because of my gluten allergy. Declining the soup was not the problem. No one minded when I brought in some gluten-free bread from the car. Toril gave me some of her homemade cloudberry jam to spread on the bread. It was delicious! The berries are kind of like raspberries, but orange, and taste more tart. I asked her where she got the berries.

"Oh, Tim!" said Roald, with mock shock (I hope it was mock). "There are three questions you must *never* ask a Norwegian: "What's your salary?", "Where do you fish for salmon?" and "Where do you pick your berries?"

We agreed to meet the next morning for a tour of nearby Senja Island. Toril declined to join us. She had plans to pick more cloudberries, and we were definitely *not* invited.

Senja is where Roald's great-grandfather came from before moving to Skøelv. His family lived on the island for at least four hundred years, perhaps more—that's just how far back their family records go. Senja is the second largest of Norway's 5,000 coastal islands. It's about 1,500 square kilometers, but with fewer than 8,000 residents, that makes it sparsely populated, with most people clustered in a few coastal fishing villages.

We drove to the end of the road at the village of Gryllefjord, which sits at the bank of a sweeping long fjord lined with jagged peaks. The ridge was formed when two glaciers ran through two parallel valleys, like two fingers of a hand. They gouged the

Left: Senja; Right: Tim, Roald and Teresa, with Skøelv in the background, across the water.

mountains between them down to a knife edge that rakes the sky. We ate lunch at a little fish restaurant run by a Thai family, and I wondered what it could possibly be like to have emigrated from one of the world's hottest countries to one of the coldest, and then to have chosen to go to the very north of that land.

Tired but happy when we returned to the mainland that evening, we said our goodbyes and thanked Roald warmly for sharing his home and childhood memories with us. Roald always stiffens for a second when we hug him, as if he's surprised. It's not very Norwegian, but he seems to like it anyway. I feel him relax. His arms curl around us in a warm bear hug. Flâmotoring around as we do, stopping here and there for a few days, it's not been easy to make new friends. For us, seeing this land through Roald's eyes has been such a gift.

We see beautiful mountains and fjords. *He* sees Dinner Mountain. *He* looks across the water to the island where his great-grandfather came from. The local bank is where his father once worked. The beach is where he and his friends played as children. The cemetery—many of the headstones bear the name Skøelv. And the old school: that building is where he discovered that he was smart, and that education could be his way out. Out, yes. But never gone. And always coming home.

Chapter 38

The Mind-Blowing Rock Art of Alta

At last Teresa and I have arrived on the north coast of Norway, the furthest north we have ever been in our lives. The Midnight Sun lasts about two and half months this far into the Arctic. And what do you suppose the weather is like? While Paris was sautéing in +40 C degree weather (104 F), we, too, were experiencing a heat wave. It was 21 C degrees (68 F) the day we arrived. I had thought I might need a winter coat in the north. But I wore a short-sleeved shirt all day.

This is not the high Arctic landscape I had anticipated: tundra and barren rock. Instead, the mountains along Norway's north shore are covered in forest, and not that much different than the coast 1,500 kilometers to the south. Why? The warm currents of

Norwegian road hazards: rocks and reindeer.

the Altantic flow up along the coast, creating more temperate weather than you find elsewhere above the Arctic Circle.

While the roads up here are few, we were surprised how good they are. Still, one should not underestimate the hazards of driving in Norway's Arctic, including falling rocks and roadside reindeer (above). (Note the collar and bell around its neck; the indigenous Sámi people domesticated reindeer some 500 years ago. That's why they are called *rein*-deer.)

After a long but spectacular drive up and down the fingers of these Arctic fjords, we eventually reached the small town of Alta at the inlet of Altafjord. It looks like a modern enough town, with a few tiny restaurants and the gleaming, silver Northern Lights Cathedral, designed around a vertical, cylindrical spire that mimicks the contours of *aurora borealis*.

Alta is one of the oldest inhabited places in Northern Europe. People first found their way to this fjord more than 7,000 years ago as the glaciers of the last Ice Age began to recede and the climate became more temperate. In fact, it was even warmer back then than it is today. These intrepid prehistoric people left evidence of settlements, arrowheads, stone tools, and, above all, carvings etched on the rocky coast of Altafjord: beautiful, mysterious, graceful works of art, thousands and thousands of them, chiseled in stone between 7,000 and 2,000 years ago.

Six thousand figures have been discovered so far at the end of Altafjord, with more being uncovered every month beneath layers of moss and lichen. The greatest concentration of them, about 3,000 etchings, are in a single open-air museum on the outskirts of town. In 1985 they were recognized as a UNESCO World Heritage Site. Walking among them on the wooden pathway was simply mind-blowing.

The most common motifs on the rocks are of animals, especially reindeer, the most numerous large mammal in the

Hunting reindeer

Arctic. Some carvings depict methods of hunting still used by the indigenous Sámi people until modern times, such as driving reindeer into an enclosure or chasing them in boats into the paths of waiting hunters (below).

The bear is also a popular figure. One rock etching depicts a mother bear with cubs, her footprints leading back to a cave. Another (below) shows a bear next to what appears to be a giant flounder at the end of a fishing line that drops from a boat. Is this some kind of spirit bear aiding the fisherman—or a simple visual aid, telling the story of landing a halibut *as big as a bear*! We will never know for sure, but it's a fact that halibut do grow this large in Arctic waters.

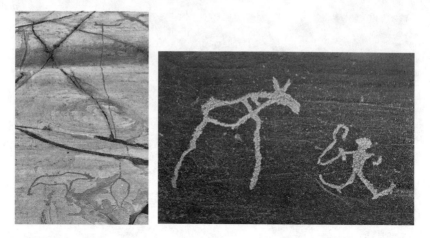

Left: Bear and halibut; Right, moose and the world's first drawing of a skier.

One of the most fascinating etchings shows a moose next to a person wearing skis—an invention attributed to the native Sámi people, and another bit of evidence supporting the Sámi claim that these lands have been their home since the dawn of history.

What became obvious to Teresa and me as we walked among the rocks is that these etched figures tell stories. Perhaps on a sunny afternoon in 5,000 B.C., one would saunter on down to the carvings and listen to one of the elders point to the bear, and tell the tale of the hunt. By encoding stories on stone, these ancient people found a way to share their practical wisdom and memorable events in a way that could be transmitted from generation to generation. That would make the rock carvings along the Alta shore the prehistoric equivalent of the Library of Alexandria, which once held all the knowledge in the ancient Mediterranean world.

Many of the carvings seem to have a mythological or symbolic element to them, so researchers think they likely had a spiritual significance as well, portraying shaman, spirit-animals, and perhaps even a comet in the sky. Since the Sámi people practiced many of the same hunting methods depicted on the rocks until modern times, it's not much of a stretch to think that their spiritual traditions of shamanism and recognition of animal spirits might also have been passed down for thousands of years from these first people who carved their stories on the rocks.

Chapter 39

Nordkapp: To the Top of Europe

Flâneur Lesson #14: The edge is everywhere

Why do some people have this impulse to go to the most extreme points on the map? Cabo de Roca—the westernmost point in mainland Europe; Cape Agulas—the southernmost point in Africa; or Norkapp—the northernmost point in mainland Europe? It's bizarre, when you think about it. A quest for the edge serves no practical purpose. And yes, Teresa and I have been to all three of these places. Nordkapp—that was yesterday.

To get there, we followed the winding fjord road along Norway's north coast, stopping for a breather in the cold, rocky harbor of Hammerfest, a community of 10,000 souls that proudly declares itself "the northernmost *town* in the world." *Town* is emphasized because there are other communities higher up, but these are not offically towns. Hammerfest seems rather strident on this point.

Hammerfest harbor was first inhabited in 1250 and became a designated town in 1838 when it served as the staging point for early polar expeditions. To commemorate this history, The Ancient Polar Bear Society was formed. I visited their free exhibition down by the docks. It's filled with memorabilia from those early Arctic journeys, with stark black and white photos of the town through the years and the first explorers. Visitors are invited to join this illustrious group. For only 35 euros you get a signed certificate with your name on it stating that you made it to Hammerfest. Plus an enamel polar bear pin. Of course, there are no actual living polar bears in

Hammerfest, and the Ancient Polar Bear Society itself is not exactly ancient. It was founded in... 1963. I didn't sign on, but I don't begrudge them offering tourists some memento of their journey.

But the *real* prize for the intrepid edge-seeker is Nordkapp. It's a long, three-hour drive from Hammerfest through mountains and fjords. The road passes through an underwater tunnel, bored deep in the bedrock to take us onto the Island of Mageroya, and right to the northernmost coast. The trees have disappeared. The land is a vast plateau of rock, covered in thin patches of green: true Arctic tundra at last.

There is, naturally, a ticket booth at the end of the road charging 30 euros per person to park and enter the visitors' center (someone has to pay for that long road to nowhere). The parking lot is full of cars and a surprising number of bicycles (I can't imagine pedaling to Norkapp in the rain). Then there are the tour buses which ferry hundreds of cruise ship passengers from the fishing village of Honningsvåg on the south shore of the island. (This fee is a great way to wring a little cash from the cruise-ship passengers who swarm Norway's tiny port towns, often buying nothing.)

At the end of the road, well, that's the end of the world. Looking north over the cliffs, we saw nothing but ocean all the way to the horizon. Luckily, we could not see the Island of Svalbard, 1,000 kilometers further north. It's part of Norway, and technically, that's the furthest-north place in Europe. So, more precisely, Nordkapp is the northernmost point in *continental* Europe.

It was freezing on the clifftop. The wind was strong. It carried the breath of ice that blew into us, no matter that it was late July.

"Finally, I feel *cold!*" exclaimed Teresa, exhilarated. Her goal for the summer has been to escape the heat. But it quickly got to be too much of a good thing. She headed for the gift shop,

Norkapp monument: The end of Europe?

leaving me to make the final walk to the modern Nordkapp monument on my own.

I watched people lining up at the monument to get their picture taken, right there at the tippy-top of the world. It's ridiculous. I tried to maintain a detached perspective on this lunacy. But I couldn't help myself. An elderly Danish man agreed to take my photo. I raised my arms in a victory pose, big foolish grin on my face.

Inside the visitors' center there's a museum about the first visitors to Nordkapp, including Francesco Negri, an Italian priest who sailed here in 1664. He was the first explorer to have Nordkapp as his final destination. Various kings have also made the journey: the king of Denmark, the king of Sweden, the kaiser of Germany, even the legendary king of Siam in 1907. Of course, before the road was finished in 1956, visitors could only arrive by ship. They had to make the steep 306-meter climb to the point of Nordkapp by foot. Even royalty had to put some effort into reaching this singular spot on the map.

Now, I imagine some alert readers have picked up the bit about us driving through an underwater tunnel. That's right,

Nordkapp is on an island. So how is that *continental* Europe? Well, you can drive to Nordkapp, so technically it is connected to the mainland. Bending definitions a bit, it could count as continental. But that's not the worst of it. For the modern pilgrim who has driven or pedaled such a long way, whatever you do, as you bask in your moment of bliss at the very furthest most north point on kind-of-continental Europe, *do not look directly to the west*! If you do, you might get a glimpse of a most-disorienting little spit of land that stretches *further north* than Nordkapp. What the....?

Well, you see it's very difficult to reach the end of that spit. Impossible to build a road there, and so, well, so, if you insist you can hike there from the road—eleven kilometers. Not even the king of Siam was up for that. So then, what does it really mean to have been to Nordkapp—to the point just next to the northernmost point on an island that is 1,000 kilometers south of the furtherest-north island of Europe?

While this instant may disorient modern pilgrims, for flâneurs it provides a potential moment of enlightenment. We embrace the reality that we did not touch the northmost point, and then rejoice because it is really all the same. The lines of latitude on a map are meaningless. What matters is we are here, right now, in freezing wind and bright Midnight Sun, feeling fully alive. And that means we can feel this alive anywhere in the world. The edge can be wherever we happen to be.

Chapter 40

Interview with a Reindeer Herder

The one time I joked about reindeer with a Sámi (pronounced Sa-ami), it was an utter disaster. I told her that the first time that Teresa and I saw a reindeer on the road we stopped and took a lot of photos. After awhile, we saw so many of them, we stopped even slowing down, and just casually pointed them out to each other ("Oh look, yet another reindeer").

"I imagine that to you, seeing a reindeer on the road is like seeing a cow is for us in North America." I gave a self-depricating laugh at our tourist foolishness.

"Reindeer are not cows," she said abruptly. "We don't milk reindeer. They are only for meat."

During the awkward pause that followed, I realized that to the Sámi, who have been hunters and herders of reindeer for thousands of years, reindeer were probably never a joking matter. Luckily, I learned this lesson a few days before meeting an actual Sámi reindeer herder.

I met Nils John at the Sápmi Cultural Park in Karasjok, one of the main centers of the Sámi in northern Norway, and the town where the Sámi built their national parliament (note: *Sápmi* is the name for traditional Sámi lands). Nils John works at the park in the summer months while his reindeer are up in the nearby mountains, fattening up on grass for the long winter ahead.

"Don't eat reindeer that's been slaughtered in the summer," he told me, within 5 minutes of our meeting. "It will make you go to the toilet."

Nils John said he took the park job because his income from herding alone was no longer enough to support his family. The reindeer in the park enclosure were part of his herd, and his teenage daughter also worked with him.

I joined a small group on Nils John's tour. The park features reconstructions of traditional Sámi summer tents—very much like the "teepees" of some North American First Nations tribes—as well as winter turf dwellings covered in sod. Nils John went into great detail about the special back part of these dwellings, where the traditional drum was kept: an item so sacred that no one was permitted to step over it. The park also contained a turf-roof, wooden winter log cabin, and a mid-twentieth-century Sámi house that would be hard to distinguish from an ordinary Norwegian home of that time.

I winced a bit when the very first question one of the tourists asked was one that even I knew you should never ask a Sámi: "How many reindeer do you own?"

"I won't answer that, because we believe it is bad luck to say it," he replied graciously. "But I can tell you my family is one of 21 families that own a herd of 6,300 reindeer."

Nils John, Sámi reindeer herder

"Do you still hunt and live in traditional ways?"

"No. Everything is modern, except the reindeer. But I don't use satellite phone or GPS. I know my land like the inside of my pocket. Even in winter when it is dark, I can shine the light from my snowmobile and see a mountain or the trees of the forest, and I know where I am."

He showed us a display of traditional winter clothing in the log house featuring reindeer-fur pants and boots of reindeer hide stuffed with dried grass for insulation. "The modern things—Gortex—they say it will keep you warm in minus 50 degrees. But it won't. If we want to wear modern clothes in winter, we wear our own clothes underneath to stay warm."

We ended the tour at an enclosure that held three of Nils John's reindeer. He fed one, and showed us how the edge of its ear had been clipped in the shape of a "W." He explained this was the identification mark for his animals. Each of the 21 families in his *siida* (a group that cooperatively manages a herd) had their own marking, as did all other reindeer herders. In his region, he could recognize 131 different ear marks. Using binoculars, any Sámi herder can tell from hundreds of meters away who owns a particular reindeer, which is extremely important when they round up the animals for sorting and slaughter at the end of the fall.

"Big Society government wants us to use an electronic barcode ear tag, like farmers use for sheep," he told us. "But to read a barcode, we have to catch the reindeer. That's a lot of effort just to find out if an animal is yours. But they don't listen to us, when we tell them it will not work..."

His tone stayed flat and matter of fact, but his frustration with "Big Society" government was easy to detect. Between tours, I had a chance to talk alone with Nils John, and he told me candidly about what he called the "dark side" of reindeer herding.

He told me the Big Society limits the size of herds so that they cannot increase. Each year the herders have to slaughter not just a certain number of animals, but also a certain number of kilograms of reindeer meat. As a result, the herders end up keeping fewer adult males, which grow the largest. But, the males also are the best foragers in winter months, and they help the females survive. Bigger and stronger males more easily dig through the snow to uncover nutritious lichen. Female reindeer often then chase the males away, and eat the lichen with their young, while the males go off and dig some more. How can the females do this? Because males lose their antlers in the fall, but the females keep theirs till spring—so they can bully the males into retreating.

"The Big Society says the herds can't grow because there's not enough food for them all," Nils John continued—and indeed, I later learned this assessment has been challenged by other researchers critical of the government's culling programs—"But at the same time, the government keeps taking more land from the reindeer. In our area, we have 2,000 square kilometers. But 800 is taken by the military, so the airforce can practice bombing. Now they want more land for wind farms. And to build more summer cabins."

I remember reading there was a real estate boom in summer cabins in Norway. I never thought Norwegians' love for the wilderness was actually *reducing* the real wilderness. And wind farms? Of course, it was easy to see how they could disturb reindeer in the mountains during the crucial summer feeding months. Reindeer tend to avoid areas where modern infrastructure is being developed.

"What about the Sámi Parliament?" I asked. "Don't your representatives raise these problems with the Norwegian government?"

"We talk, but they don't listen," he said in the same flat tone.

"All three of my children want to become reindeer herders," he continued. "But the government says only one person in each family can inherit a permit to herd. The other two will have to go to school, get a job in a town..."

It seemed to me as if the Norwegian government was slowly squeezing the Sámi herders, while the needs of the Big Society just grow and grow.

It's true that after centuries of persecuting and oppressing the Sámi, Norway has gone further than other Scandinavian nations in providing space for the Sámi to recover their identity and express themselves. But. But. Norway presents itself to the world as a socially progressive and environmentally conscious nation. Yet, apparently they are not listening to what the Sámi tell them about their herds and the land that is their home. Currently, the Sámi Parliament can only make *suggestions* to Norway's government. What the Sámi are seeking is veto power over legislation affecting the Sámi people that they disagree with.

I later read a research article on Sámi reindeer herding that put it like this: To the Norwegian government, reindeer herding is about meat production. But animal husbandry is only a part of what reindeer mean to the Sámi. To tag a reindeer like you would tag a sheep, to regulate them by the kilo: this is being blind not only to the culture and spiritual values of the Sámi people, but also to the ecological values the reindeer and their herders bring to this fragile Arctic ecosystem.

I hope somewhere in Big Society, someone is listening.

This beautiful male was worth stopping for on the road. White reindeer are seen as special to the Sámi, because they tend not to follow the herd: they find their own path.

Chapter 41

Who Are the Sámi People?

Teresa and I started our journey through Norway with next to zero information about the Sámi. The little we knew came from TV shows about Vikings and wilderness survival, so we were probably more misinformed than informed. We've spent the past two weeks not just in Sámi territory, but in their front room—the towns and villages with the largest Sámi populations in Norway. Teresa and I have visited the Sámi Parliament building—made of native wood and built to blend into the surroundings—and we've been to pretty much every Sámi museum in the region. We've had a few good face-to-face conversations along the way. Perhaps our biggest

My photo of a Sámi family from 1920, taken from a tourist info sign by the roadside.

misperception was that we thought the Sámi were related to either the Inuit of North America or Asians. And so, on meeting blonde-haired blue-eyed Sámi—not just one, but many—we were a bit dis-oriented, so to speak.

Sámi genetics studies have shown that they are *not* related to Asians. Several thousand years ago, they migrated to Scandinavia from the Ural Mountains, which mark the boundary between Europe and Asia. And so, not only are they Europeans, they are very *old* Europeans. Their distinct genetic heritage is matched with a distinct Uralic language (a linguistic root shared only with Finns, Hungarians and Estonians).

While populations rose and fell in the rest of Europe, developed agriculture, warfare, city-states, politics, the Sámi stayed relatively clear of it all by moving further and further north. Once, they were mostly in central Finland, but migrated *up* as the people we call Scandinavians today encroached on their territories from the south. It used to be thought that the Sámi were descended from the Finns, but today it is accepted that the Finns are a hybrid between Sámi and north-migrating Europeans.

While some Sámi retain the traditional livelihoods of fishing and reindeer herding, most of the 100,000 of them live and work much as their "Big Society" neighbors do. They are artists, politicians, business professionals, academics, hairdressers and teachers.

But, importantly, after centuries of cultural oppression, many Sámi have recovered a strong sense of identity and pride in their heritage. At the Kautokieno Museum, near the northern border of Finland, I met a young Sámi man who worked there. The museum was quiet the day I visited, so Johann and I talked for about an hour about what growing up Sámi has meant to him.

Johann. I wanted to take his picture in the museum, and asked him to take me to his favorite exhibit. He chose these 200-year-old carved wooden bowls. This is the kind of carving he likes to do himself, and he admires the artistry and longevity of these bowls his ancestors made.

Johann told me that the old three-roomed wooden house on display in the outdoor part of the museum is actually his great-grandparents' home, which was moved from its location in the nearby mountains. The house is famous in Kautokieno because near the end of WWII, the Russians invaded northern Norway. As the occupying Nazi forces fled, they burned everything to the ground, and attempted to remove everyone from the region, so that the Russians would find nothing but a wasteland. Many Sámi fled into the wilderness. Thirty of them found their way to Johann's ancestral home, where they were welcomed by his great-grandparents and sheltered through the long, harsh winter.

Johann is studying for his Masters at the Sámi Univeristy in Kautokieno. I asked what he wants to do with his life. He said he enjoys hand-carving bowls and utensils using "hard materials"—wood and reindoor antler. But what he will probably do as a profession is become a teacher, likely a Sámi language teacher at the local middle school. He seemed pretty certain that although he has enjoyed international travel— several trips through Europe, and one to Toronto for a global conference for indigenous youth—Kautokieno is where he wants to build his life.

Johann filled me with hope for the Sámi. He's a man who knows his past, and knows the world: a man who chooses to build a better future for his people, so that they may find their place in the world without losing their identity.

Chapter 42

The Drum Who Came Home

To the Sámi people, their ritual drums are not simply cultural artifacts. They are "powerful non-human beings." So the very first repatriation of a drum back to Sámi territory, after being taken exactly 330 years ago by Danish authorities, is a big deal. It happened in January 2022. In July, I saw this drum on display at the Sámi museum in Karasjok, not far from the Sámi Parliament. The drum rests in a spotlit, glass case in its own separate, darkened room. It is the only item in the whole museum that visitors are not allowed to photograph.

The story of this drum—its biography, if you like—is told in vivid detail in the adjoining room, together with an explanation of the instrumental role drums played in traditional Sámi culture. Here's what the museum placard has to say about the process of repatriation:

The return of our sacred drums will promote Sámi self-identification, strengthen self-esteem, and restore the broken ties to our history and to the world of our ancestors. All over Sámpi, drums are described as the means of communications between people and the world of spirits... The sacred drums were taken from the Sámi without their consent. The drums shall no longer be stowed away in the warehouses of European mega-museums or to be exhibited as obscure curiosities from the Arctic. Drums are not merely objects for use, but rather they are considered powerful non-human beings with their own will and with a voice. Therefore, the exhibition presents the drums with respect, as persons. Their life stories are told as biographies. In this way, the drums are coming home. After centuries of voiceless time and silence, the drums are once again getting a voice.

These "powerful non-human beings with their own will and voice" played a crucial role in the lives of the Sámi: foretelling weather, the movement of reindeer herds, the best times to hunt, how to heal sicknesses and help women in childbirth. Noidi (shaman) could play their drums to induce a trance state and travel to the spirit world, where they could gather wisdom or intercede for those in need.

I like to keep an open mind about ways of knowing that are beyond my own horizons. In trying to grasp the multifaceted

Sámi *noidi* (shaman) with a drum. My photo from the Varjjat Museum on the Varanger Penninsula.

role of the drum in the context of my own culture, the closest I could get was a Smart Phone—that is, if we believed Siri or Alexa or Hey Google were sentient beings we communicated with that connected us to some vast ether-like "cloud" of information.

I'm saying this as a joke, of course. But I do believe it's possible the Sámi used their drums to tap into sources of information that reductionist Western science can't yet fathom, just as we don't grasp how salmon return to the stream in which they were spawned, or how some animals seem to sense an earthquake hours before it happens. Evolutionary scientists are discovering that even at the molecular level of DNA, there seems to be a level of perception, connection and communication we have yet to understand.

Anders Poulsen was the Sámi noidi who owned the drum who returned to Karasjok. The museum also tells his story. In brief: In 1692 Poulsen was charged with the crime of witchcraft, specifically for possessing and using a drum. This was at the end of a century that saw 91 women and men tried and executed for witchcraft in the northeastern Arctic town of Vardø. Most were burned at the stake. (The Salem Witch Trials that killed 25 people in Massachusetts also took place in this time period.)

At his trial, Poulsen freely admitted he used the drum, and gave detailed testimony as to the meanings of all the symbols it contained. He also explained how he used the drum only for good: to advise, protect and heal those who came to him for help. For this, the court sentenced him to death. But the judge delayed the ruling, waiting for the authorities in Denmark (the rulers of Norway at the time) to weigh in. Poulsen's relatives pleaded for mercy, urging again and again that the old man never did any harm. Poulsen was murdered in his cell the day after the trial by the sheriff's deputy. Historical accounts call that deputy "deranged." To me, he seemed incentivized.

Poulsen's drum was taken to Denmark and added to the private collection of the king, who apparently would beat on it for amusement from time to time. It ended up in the Danish National Museum. In 1972 it was sent, *on loan*, to the museum in Karasjok. Only in 2022, due to efforts of the Danish royal family, was it finally repatriated to the Sámi people.

Poulsen's story is just one tragic example of the centuries-long campaign to destroy Sámi culture and religion. The Sámi were, in fact, the last people in Europe to be "Christianized." Their drums were taken away. Many drums were burned and destroyed as tools of the devil. Others were sent to museums throughout Scandinavia and the world. Of the seventy or so thought to be in existence today, Poulsen's is the only drum who has come home.

Progress is being made, but there's a long way to go. Norway is a signatory of the UN Declaration on the Rights of Indigenous Peoples. Like Canada, the US, and Australia, Norwegians are still trying to come to terms with the brutal treatment of their indigenous people—policies once labeled "Norwegianization." In 1997, King Harald V of Norway publicly apologized to the Sámi people for the repression they suffered under Norwegian rule.

The Sámi in Norway now have their own democratically elected parliament. It's a governing body for their own cultural affairs, and can also make "suggestions" to Norway's central government. The Sámi aim, however, is to gain actual veto rights on legislation that directly affects them. That does not seem too much to ask. A Sámi man told me his people know they have better representation in Norway than their kin do in Sweden or Finland. And that all of them are much better off than the Sámi living in northwestern Russia.

The Norwegian government recently promised to return some 2,000 Sámi items held in Norwegian museums to Karasjok.

And four other drums are in the process of being returned from other museums in Northern Europe.

One of the Karasjok museum staff told me their director was currently visiting the Smithsonian Institute in Washington D.C., supervising the 3-D scanning of Sámi artifacts the museum had acquired, including two drums. This process allows for 3-D printing of replicas, and it can be an important step in the eventual return of "taken" articles to their rightful homeland. For the Sámi, it is more than returning stolen possessions. It is returning stolen heritage, stolen parts of themselves—some of whom are drums.

Chapter 43

In Svalbard, I Want to Hug a Walrus

I had never heard of Svalbard before Teresa started planning our trip to Norway. Located about 1,000 km north of mainland Norway, and about 1,000 km south of the North Pole, Svalbard lies on the same latitude as the north coast of Greenland. It is not one island, but a whole frozen *archipelago,* 60% covered in ice, and contains the third-largest icecap on the planet (after Antarctica and Greenland).

The one town on the island, Longyearbyen, has a population of about 2,300 people. It's the northermost town in the entire world. We recalled *Fortitude*—a British *Arctic Noir* thriller series set in a fictional, far northern island that featured stars such as Stanley Tucci and Dennis Quaid. I checked, and indeed, fictional *Fortitude* is based loosely on real-world Longyearbyen, and some of the show was filmed on location.

Longyearbyen, with its glacier in the background.

How the hell do you even get to such a remote and forbidding place? To our surprise, there are daily flights from Oslo and Tromsø (the Arctic capital of Norway). We parked our Polestar 2 at the Tromsø airport and took off. We didn't know what to expect.

Svalbard is polar bear territory. In fact, one local regulation is that you can't leave the town limits without a gun in case you meet a hungry bear. The three roads at the ends of town each have a triangular caution marker warning that you are going outside the polar bear safe zone. It's no joke; a hiker was attacked on Svalbard while we were visiting the island. (The bear came into her tent and mauled her. The guides shot at it and scared it way. She suffered a broken arm; the bear was tracked down by helicopter, determined to be badly wounded, and killed.)

When we checked into our hotel, the Funken Lodge (more swanky than funky), we were given the polar bear briefing by a cheerful young Irish woman named Lisa. She told us bears only wander inside the town itself a *couple of times a year*. "So, if you see a bear, immediately run into the closest house or car. Everyone in town is very trusting, and no one locks their doors," she said with a smile.

It dawned on me that there was really no such thing as a polar bear safe zone in Svalbard. The bears could not read the posted signs.

The town itself is surreal. It's located in a glacial mountain valley that seems just recently vacated by the glacier, which lurks a few kilometers up the valley. The gray shale hills have a slight sheen of green tundra on their lower slopes. The tops disappear into the fog.

The bare land, scraped clean by the retreating ice, seems raw and unformed, as if newly made. But that's an illusion. The hillsides are shot with the shafts of abandonned coal mines, dug over the past 100 years. Coal—carbonized vegetation—in a land of ice? How is that possible? The island was tropical forest millions of years ago, when the continents were much differently arranged. This land is not brand new; it's merely the current incarnation that makes it seem so raw. Dinosaur fossils abound.

The modern town is built on the remains of the coal town, though much was destroyed in WWII when the Nazis bombed it. So the buildings are all relatively new. The place has a Wild West feel to it, as if there was never any city planning and the town evolved in haphazard clumps. Because the land is permafrost (frozen solid just a few feet below the surface) all the buildings are set up on stilts. The water and electrical cables run alongside the streets above ground as well. Everywhere there are snowmobiles on wooden pallets, waiting for winter to return.

Weathered and broken wooden towers criss-cross the valley and town, slowly decaying. These used to support cables that ferried buckets of coal from the mines down to the port. Now they are designated heritage monuments and cannot be removed, even though they look as if they might collapse at any moment. The old mining barracks are similarly protected sites, as is a small miners' graveyard, marked with 37 white crosses.

It's because of these early graves that it is now illegal to die in Svalbard. Those who perished from mining accidents decades ago and are buried get pushed back up to the surface from time to time by the permafrost. What's worse, the cold keeps their bodies from decomposing! Rather than put up with this attempted zombie behavior, back in 1950 the authorities decided to fly people to the mainland if they fall terminally ill. Technically a corpse could be cremated on the island, but there's no demand for funeral services, hence no crematorium.

If Longyearbyen billed itself as a historic mining town, I imagine few people would come all this way for a visit. But in the past few decades the town has reinvented itself as an ecotourism destination. Indeed, as soon as we arrived we signed ourselves up for a different tour every day.

Our first full day on the island, we headed out on an electric catamaran across *Isfjorden* (literally, "Ice-fjord") to a massive glacier that flows from the ice cap. Our goal for the trip: walrus spotting. Our guide was a vivacious, young Russian named Katerina. She enthusiastically told us all about walruses on our way across the fjord. Males grow bigger than polar bears, and weigh up to two metric tons (4,400 pounds). They use their tusks not only for fighting, but to help them stir up mollusks from the seabed when they feed. They also use their tusks to pull themselves onto ice flows, like a climber might use an ice-axe. For this reason, one of their names is "Tooth Walker."

"Walrus are a kind of monster, it's true," Katerina told us with a smile. "But they are also quite cute!"

She said they like to congregate together on beaches, and as they prefer to stick to the same locations, they are pretty easy to find by boat.

"They like to feel cosy," Katerina said. "They need phyical contact with others to be happy. Zoos found that single walruses don't do well. They get depressed. So in some cases, their caretakers' job includes giving the lonesome walruses a lot of hugs."

We found the walruses right by the shore, perhaps a dozen of them, massive caramel-colored rolls of fat, topped with tusks, all snuggled together. A few of the smaller ones shuffled into the water, splashing around as if playing. We kept our distance, but they hardly seemed to notice us. They seemed pretty chill. Walruses received protective status in Norway in 1952, after 350 years of unregulated slaughter by hunters in Svalbard almost wiped them out.

In the days that followed, I kayaked in the fjord and hiked on the hills, always in a group, and always with an armed guide. On our fourth day we took it easy and signed up for a two-hour city tour in a van. Our guide, Vigo, was a Norwegian airforce vet with a great sense of humor. He told us he's the second oldest resident on Svalbard. He filled us in on what the guidebooks all too often gloss over about the town's history. Here are the highlights:

- March 8 is the day the sun returns to Svalbard after three and a half months of darkness. They call it *Sun*day. The town celebrates with a party that lasts for a week.
- Norway has only run Svalbard since 1925. The post-war Treaty of Versailles granted a reluctant Norway the responibility of administering the islands on behalf of 25 nations that signed the agreement. Citizens of those nations still have the right to enter Svabard and live here, visa free, provided they have a job that can sustain them, and they can find a place to live. Currently, people from 52 countries live here.
- Norway can't collect taxes on residents of Svalbard, except for a 16% income tax only for municipal use. As a result, many things are cheaper here than in the rest of Norway, including alcohol.
- The polar ice is melting, fast. Vigo told us a Danish research vessel was here this summer. They were cruising to the North Pole and had allotted two weeks to get through the sea ice on the journey. Instead, it took them only two days.
- Polar bears seem to be leaving Svalbard. According to Vigo, in 2015 there were around 3,000 bears, but most recent counts put the total at around 925. They need sea ice to hunt seals, their main prey, and as the ice is melting due to climate change, the bears (Vigo figures) are probably migrating across the Arctic sea ice to Canada, where it is much colder.

- A network of domed antennas receive satellite signals on a plateau above the airport. As Vigo explained, the earth is a bit flattened out at the poles, and not a perfect globe. So signals have a much wider reach up here. The island gathers a massive amount of satellite data. For this reason, NASA paid over 90% of the cost of installing two undersea fiber-optic cables that run from the Norwegian mainland, so they could capture that data. As a nice byproduct, there's fast Internet connectivity for everyone on the island, which is why we can watch Netflix and I can write a blogpost from Svalbard.

- Since Svalbard is so strategically important, Norway has decided to strengthen its stake here by making Longyearbyen a more permanent settlement. Whereas decades ago the town used to be mostly transient miners, today it is a "family town" with three schools and so many children that the average age is 30 years old. It's got a library, sportsplex, hospital, church, grocery story, more than a dozen restaurants, and its own radio station.

- Longyearbyen is home to the World Seed Vault, a "back-up bank" buried in a mountainside that contains the genetic diversity of millions of crops—including over 200,000 varieties of wheat. The seeds are stored below the permafrost level, to keep them cold so they will never spoil. If a disaster wipes out a crop, these seeds can be retrieved and the crop restored. It's a global insurance policy for future generations. And *not* open to the public.

Perhaps the most intriguing thing about Svalbard is the people who come here to make a living. Most come for a season and end up staying on average 3–10 years. Sure, many leave for the south during the three months of winter darkness. But there's work here even when it's forty-below freezing and storms last

Left: A flâneur attempts to break into the global seed vault. Right: Vigo explains all about Svalbard.

for weeks. Companies run Northern Lights tours for tourists, and dogsled rides. In our short five days we met a Czech social anthropologist, a Malaysian taxi driver, a multilingual French guide, a Ukrainian mixologist, a Thai barista, and, of course, Katerina the Russian walrus guide. The Funken Lodge front desk was manned by an Englishman, an Irishwoman and a Finn! They each had their reasons for coming here, and probably quite different ones for deciding to stay.

Could Svalbard be home for us some day? It's a tantalizing thought, moving to this Wild West town in the far north. So legally easy, with no visa requirement, but so logistically intimidating. Perpetual daylight all summer long, then darkness for three solid months. It's a dream of a life so different from anything we have known. What would we do? Teach at the school? Join Vigo on the tour bus? Mix cocktails at the Funken Lodge? Work on polar bear conservation? On Svalbard, anything seems possible.

Chapter 44

Letting Go on Lofoten

We are not exactly wasting away in Margaritaville, but Teresa and I are loafing a ton on Lofoten, the famous island chain in Norway's western Arctic. On the morning of day nine here, it's pouring rain. Yay! Once more the mist has rolled in over the mountains and onto the rocky shore, right down to the cod-drying racks of our little fishing village of Ballstad. The sea is dark and calm. Beneath the clear surface, patches of aquamarine reveal white sand interspersed with dark clumps of kelp, home to crabs and sea urchins. Teresa and I will stay inside our little red cabin today. Unless the sky clears and the mountain roads beckon. Maybe we will spy sea eagles again?

For two months we have been driving around Norway in our zippy Polstar 2. Norwegians we have met along the way tell us we have seen more of their country than they have. It's been glorious. We feel we have truly hit our stride as flâneurs, wandering around with no purpose other than to experience the beauty of the Arctic. But even wanderers get weary moving from place to place, three days here, five days there. So after Svalbard we decided to take a vacation from our vacation and stay put in Lofoten for 12 days.

The Lofoten islands are ideally suited for a laid-back lifestyle. Frankly, there is not a lot to do. Hiking, kayaking, a few boat tours. Same-same as in the rest of Norway. What there is, however, is an abundance of spectacularity. In a land of endless mountains, Lofoten manages to stand out. Driving the one main road through the island chain, one finds breathtaking beauty around every bend.

Lofoten

You might think the very gorgeousness of this place would be its ruin, that Lofoten was at risk of becoming over-touristed: part Yellowstone, part Nantucket, part Disneyland. But that has not happened. Two or three villages do seem mostly given over to tourists, but about 99% of Lofoten remains its age-old self: fishing hamlets in the shelter of rocky harbors; farmsteads in the shadows of mountains. It's a legacy that goes back more than a thousand years to Viking times.

In fact, the major tourist attraction is the Lofoten Viking Museum. It stands on a hilltop on the island of Vestvågøy. The heart of it is an archeological site that includes the largest Viking longhouse in all of Scandinavia. It's 83 meters (272 feet) from end to end. Right next to these ancient foundations a full-scale reproduction has been constructed that looks as big as Noah's Ark. Inside, several Viking-costumed actors sit around weaving, carving or performing other Viking-appropriate tasks.

Of course, their main job is to chat with the tourists about what life was like back in the good old days.

Although archeological evidence is scant at the site (the Vikings used mostly wood, wool and leather, which disintegrate over time), the Old Norse Book of Settlements tells the story of a chieftain from Lofot who likely owned this longhouse in the 900s. Here's what the museum website has to say about him:

> The chieftain was called Olaf Tvennumbruni. He was described as a great man of sacrifices and a "hamram". This means that he led the Norse sacrificial ceremonies and gave great feasts in honour of the gods. "Hamram" means that the people believed he could shed his skin and transform himself into an animal....

I'll interject here: The Norse had a profoundly spiritual sense of connection with certain power animals: wolf, bear, boar, eagle and serpent. They believed special individuals could not only absorb the power of their spirit animal but could become physically transformed into it—something like a werewolf. To continue from the website:

> The Chieftain's House was abandoned in the 900s. We do not know why, but this was a time of great upheaval. Power structures were changing as a result of both the unification of Norway as a nation and the Christianisation process. We know that several great chieftains resettled in Iceland towards the end of the Viking Age.

That, apparently, is what Olaf did. He moved to Iceland rather than compromise his independence under the new king of a united Norway. Nor could he bow to a religion that might not have dealt kindly with a werewolf, I suppose.

One of the Viking actors at the museum, a young woman weaver in an embroidered blue dress, told me the Lofoten community feels intense pride that they have the longest longhouse in the world.

"Earlier this summer, a big longhouse was discovered in Denmark," she told me. "We were quite worried at first. Then, they determined it was just 63 meters long. 'Ah, how cute!' we said. 'You could put that one *inside* our longhouse!'" She gave a satisfied smile, then added, "I guess you can say when it comes to longhouses, size does matter."

The reconstructed longhouse features a dining hall, where they put on Viking feasts with costumed actors every evening. Next to it, remembering Olaf's sacrifices to the gods, there's a room with a model of Yggdrasill, the World Tree, that connects the nine realms of Viking cosmology. The museum also includes a reconstructed Viking longship you can sail on in the nearby fjord, and every August they hold a week-long Viking festival. These are all irresistible, family-friendly options. Kids can even try on some Viking armor. I wonder, how exactly did Vikings become so "kid-friendly"? I guess that like pirates and dinosaurs, it's the *savagery* that children find so fascinating.

Other than hanging with the Vikings, we mostly drove through the fjords and mountain valleys, exploring a different island each day, awestruck by the changing colors of the hills, and the mist that sweeps like cascading water across the peaks. There are, however, a few surprising places worth mentioning:

The old fishing village of Å (pronounced "o" as in "old") is at the end of the road on the Isle of Moskenesöya. The E10 highway literally stops at the Å parking lot. Beyond that, there are only mountains and a few rocky islets leading out to the Atlantic. Å is filled with quaint, restored nineteenth-century homes that seem so incongruously formal and tidy against the stark cliffs at their back. One of these houses has been converted into a bakery that serves only one thing: cinnamon buns. "11 out of 10," is how Teresa rates them. "The best cinnamon buns I have had in my entire life," she says.

The village also has a good restaurant and two museums. One is devoted entirely to dried cod. Perhaps that seems hard to fathom. But just north of Lofoten is the most abundant cod fishery in the world. Dried cod has been the mainstay of the Lofoten economy for over a thousand years. Vikings (like Olaf) used to trade Lofoten cod as far south as Spain.

Ramberg Beach, on Moskenesöya island, is one of several white-sand beaches that seem so incongruous in Lofoten's cold climate. They look like they belong in the Caribbean. But don't be fooled. We only ever saw two people swim in these chilly waters. One woman, wearing a wetsuit, lasted less than two minutes. The other, however, frolicked like a seal in nothing but her bathing suit and cap. Perhaps she was a local mermaid?

Lofoten Links Golf Course. When we saw the signs on the windswept north coast of Gimsøya Isle, we thought this golf course was an elaborate joke. We observed tees and greens, but in between, the rough looked pretty rough! Here's what their website has to say: "Lofoten Links is a spectacular 18-hole links course... located by the seaside with an unobstructed view to the North and the midnight sun. Playing and walking the course is a grand experience where the ocean is a water hazard on several holes and sandy beaches act as natural bunkers." I know it sounds like hyperbolic marketing, but honestly, what golfer could resist playing a round under the midnight sun?

Henningsvær Harbor. Tourists have definitely discovered this adorable fishing village tucked into a tiny island off the south coast of Austvågöy Island. Fresh fish and seafood restaurants abound, and brightly painted souvenir shops and art boutiques line the pedestrian lane that winds through the village center. Tour boats putter and kayaks glide through the harbor. It's kind of nice to have the touristy bits all kept so compact, like a honey pot attracting all the flies. We buzzed around quite happily ourselves for an hour or two.

Postscript: The wind is up on our last morning in Lofoten. There's a sea eagle flying round the cliffs, so close we can see her white tail feathers twitch as she steadies herself in the buffeting wind. We wonder how wild our ride will be on the ferry ride to Bodø this afternoon, across open water. The thought is a bit unnerving. But, like our Polestar 2, our batteries are fully recharged. We are ready to pack up and get back on the road.

At the same time, a sadness wells up at the thought of leaving. It turns out, letting go *on* Lofoten is easier than letting go *of* Lofoten. I want to hold these mountains in my mind's eye so that they stay alive in me when I'm gone. It's a weird feeling, like homesickness for a place I have not yet left. Teresa feels it too. We have agreed that this is good information, this feeling. You see, after nine months of flâneuring, we don't really know where home is anymore. So, if our hearts ache when we leave a place, it's because it feels like home. Lofoten, we will be back.

Chapter 45

Vikings versus Flâneurs

One of the things I've enjoyed most about Norway is learning about the Vikings in their own land. The traveler in me always loved tales of the Northmen (and Northwomen) who voyaged far and wide a thousand years ago, not only to new lands—Iceland, Greenland and North America—but all the way south down the Atlantic coast to the Mediterranean Sea, and also inland by river from the Baltic Sea through Russia and Ukraine to the Black Sea and Constantinople. While indeed they pillaged, the Vikings were traders more than raiders. In

A modern-day Viking on the loose in Oslo. The horns were never part of Viking armor.

connecting Scandinavia to the wealth of southern lands, they knitted together a whole continent that had fallen apart in the centuries since the unraveling of the Roman Empire.

Do we really have anything in common, flâneurs and Vikings? I decided to do a brief analysis of similarities and differences between these two very different types of travelers.

Sense of Purpose

One thing you can say about Vikings, they were purposeful. Whether exploring or trading, conquering or raiding, they always had a goal in mind when they set off for a distant land. Look at Ganger Rolf (below) pointing to the north of France, the land he is about to invade and conquer—known as *Normandy* ("North-man-land") to this day.

The city of Rouen, in Normandy, France, gifted this statue to the town of Ålesund, where Ganger Rolf was born.

Flâneurs, however, amble under a different banner: a banner of frivolity. Having no particular purpose is central to the whole enterprise. To simply be in the moment and enjoy the scenery is enough for us. Imagine, if you will, what it would be like for a flâneur to hitch a ride on a Viking longship. First, all that rowing, day after day, would not go down well. Second, the flâneur would want to stop and explore some of the prettier coves along the way. Marauding—that sounds like so much effort! And why do we have to break stuff and take stuff! Just take a photo and Instagram it, Ganger Rolf!

Impact

When the Vikings came to town, everyone knew it. If they came as traders, they brought with them for barter narwal tusks and walrus ivory, reindeer pelts, and most important of all, dried cod—a fantastic and long-lasting source of protein. If they came

This catastrophe is what happens when a flâneur plays Viking.

as raiders, they left devastation in their wake, and carried away plundered gold and silver.

Flâneurs travel lightly. We are not interested in collecting gold and jewels to add to the hoard, maybe just the occasional souvenir T-shirt (though Teresa might disagree with me about the jewels). Leaving behind a memorable conversation, or perhaps the occasional generous tip, is all the impact we seek.

Community

The Vikings were a most communal people. You can't row a Viking longship all by yourself, nor can you storm the walls of York, nor conquer Normandy. In Lofoten we walked through a full-scale reproduction of a Viking longhouse, and marveled at how very communal Viking life must have been. There were large spaces for banqueting and entertainment, work spaces for artisans, storage for dried fish and animal fodder, even areas decorated with totems of the gods, marked out for sacred rituals. Every facet of life went on within these walls. And no wonder: winters were long, dark and cold. Of course, people wanted to stay warm and safe together.

Flâneurs are not communal. Social, yes. We love to visit, to dive into the center of things, but then just as quickly hop out and move along to whatever comes next. Friends and family are important to our lives, but we don't have to live right next door.

Solitude

The flip side of loving community, however, is the ability to be alone. Exile was the worst punishment you could inflict on a Viking—worse than death. I remember a long time ago reading an Old Norse poem from one of the Viking sagas, voiced by one such Viking exile, expressing not only his grief, but also the soul-crushing sorrow he felt living in isolation.

But solitude is the companion of the flâneur: one who wanders alone and adrift. He—or she—wants for nothing and seeks only the stimulation of his curiosity, and perhaps the occasional glass of Chablis. While indeed Teresa and I are the rare flâneurs-au-deux, a twosome is not at all what a Viking longs for in community. In short, the flâneur is not simply the opposite of the Viking, the flâneur lives the kind of life *the Viking most fears*!

Now, I get it that this love for community has probably become, a thousand years later, the main reason Scandinavian nations are the most advanced social democracies in the world, with the highest levels of happiness and the lowest levels of crime on the planet. As a flâneur, I am happy for them, and also I benefit directly, because I get to travel easily through countries that are safe, modern, and courteous, with great infrastructure and where everyone speaks English—because the education system is well funded and prepares the next generation for life in an interconnected global world.

And this brings me to my final comparison:

Curiosity

The Vikings were ready to sail off the map, or head for lands far away, sometimes on the basis of the faintest of rumors. That kind of curiosity is at the heart of what it means to be a flâneur. I was gobsmacked, in fact, to discover that the French word *flâneur* actually derived from an Old Norse term *flana*, which meant "to wander," or to paraphrase more explicitly, "to explore without knowing exactly what you are looking for." I found it truly astonishing the number of Norwegians we met who shared that flana-flâneuring sense of curious adventure. Almost every conversation with a Norwegian—even with hotel clerks, waiters and grocery store cashiers—began with the question, "Where are you from?" Almost inevitably, they would follow up our answer by telling us where they had been, which was usually to the US, Canada, Australia, or "down south to Europe." They see themselves as Norwegians first, but also as global citizens.

That love of exploration left me with a sweet sense of kinship as we flâneured among these tall, blonde, healthy folk whose bold, ferocious ancestors had changed the course of history.

Chapter 46

Røros: A Charming Town with a Dirty Past

We knew we wanted to visit the historic copper mining town of Røros years before Teresa and I planned our trip to Norway. While most towns have modernized over the years, Røros has meticulously preserved its traditional wooden houses; it's like stepping into a historical film set. For this, it's been designated as a UNESCO World Heritage Site. The town is most famous for how the residents do Christmas. As it says on the town website, "Røros is not decorated for Christmas—Røros *is* Christmas!" When it snows, the streets don't get cleared: they stay covered in a soft white blanket. People ski through town or kick-push themselves along on sledges—basically a cross between a scooter and a sled. The old wooden houses—gaily painted in reds, greens, yellows, or varnished so that the dark exposed timbers gleam beneath red-trimmed roofs—are all lit up with colored lights. There's a Christmas market, and the whole town turns into a Christmas card.

Røros was featured in Netflix's first Norwegian series, *Hjem til Jul* (*Home for Christmas*, in English), which is how Teresa and I first heard of the town. It's the hilarious tale of a 30-year-old nurse named Johanne who works in Røros. She keeps getting put at the children's table at her parents' home during their traditional Christmas Eve dinner because she is the only adult sibling in her family without a partner. In order to avoid this humiliation yet again, in early December the plucky but unlucky Johanne sets out to find a boyfriend before Christmas. Hilarity ensues, along with guffaw-inducing sexual hi-jinx. Who knew Norwegians could be so funny? The show showcases the best

Christmas scenes of Røros. On-screen, the town looks absolutely enchanting.

Even though we arrived in late summer on our drive south from the Arctic, Røros had us at "hei-hei" (Norwegian for "hello"). We drove through the main streets and immediately fell for the gorgeously kept rows of antique houses. Teresa had booked us into an Airbnb in one of the historic homes, a 200-year-old wooden house built with thick, sturdy beams over a slate floor. Even the furniture was all old wood: handmade chests, heavy beds, and tables. As we toured the four large rooms that would be ours for three days we felt as if we were living back in the 1800s.

Our hostess, Maren, told us because this was a designated historic house, it could not be modernized or altered, other than by adding electric wiring. So, no indoor plumbing? Well, no. But the bathrooms were connected across a corridor in another part of the compound. This made for nightly adventures in the dark, feeling our way down uneven wooden stairs and over slate floors to distant toilet seats.

The kitchen featured a massive open fireplace in the corner. It had a traditional Norwegian design with a large whitewashed chimney that took up a full corner of the room. A fire was going when we arrived and we could see how well the chimney sucked up all the smoke. The open, slate-covered area around the fire was so wide, that there was no risk of sparks flying and flames spreading. Maren, told us, nonchalantly, that we could leave the house with the fire going, no problem.

After a stroll through the old town, Teresa gushed, "This is my favorite place in Norway!" (and Teresa's not a gusher). I asked, what pulled her heartstrings so?

"It's the careful attention to beautiful details in all the houses and shops."

I saw it too: the flourishes in the façades, pots of colorful flowers set out by the doorways, the whimsical statues, or hand-painted works of art. It seemed as if the whole town devoted itself not just to preserving their heritage, but to celebrating it. This attention to detail is part of what has made Røros such a popular holiday getaway for Norwegians, and not just at Christmas time. It's also a major wedding destination. On our second day there, a wedding was held in the 350-year-old town church up on the hill, overlooking the town.

Just a few blocks from the church is the mining museum, housed in the town's defunct copper smelter. It is also part of the UNESCO World Heritage Site. Across the cheerful little river from the museum are the Røros slag heaps: thousands of tons of pulverized brown-red rock that was processed to remove the copper ore. The heaps rise more than fifty meters high, like massive, reddish-black sand dunes on which nothing grows. They fill an area roughly the size of an Olympic stadium. They

Two of Teresa's favorite vignettes of Røros

are *also* part of the UNESCO site. Signs warn visitors not to take any slag from the heap. No souvenirs!

The copper works are not simply part of Røros' history, it is the very reason for the town's existence. When copper deposits were discovered in the area in the mid-1600s, the king of Denmark (who ruled Norway at that time), granted a mining company (which became the Røros Copper Works) royal permission to exploit all the resources within a 40 km radius— in return for a 10% share of the profits. The king also gave the company the right to compel farmers within that region to work for the new mine. Soon the town of Røros was built up near the smelter, where the extracted ore was processed.

The process of mining copper involved not just digging up rock, but heating it, cracking it, and smelting it to separate the metal from the raw ore. The town—this shiny Christmas town— was usually submerged in a cloud of dust and sulphuric smoke from the smelter. It would fill the air and choke the inhabitants, until a smokestack was finally built in 1901, to send the fumes high into the sky instead.

To make heat hot enough for smelting they needed charcoal from burned wood. The forests around Røros were quickly chopped down for fuel. Soon, it became more economical to build new smelters in virgin forests and haul the raw ore overland from the mines. Those new forests were, in turn, devoured to feed the smelters, and before more modern sources of heat were found, the entire 40 km radius of land, and more, had been cut clear of trees.

I try to imagine how this destruction must have appeared to the Southern Sámi, who had lived sustainably on this land for thousands of years, hunting and herding reindeer. The museum includes a model of a Sámi stone hearth found near Røros that dates from Viking times. What must the Sámi have thought about the insatiable need of these new outsiders to demolish the whole forest in order to melt rocks for the shiny red substance hidden inside?

From all this effort, 110,000 tonnes of copper were produced between 1644 and 1977 to become copper coins, copper roofs, copper pots, and later, copper wire. A few men became very wealthy. Then in the 1970s, after several years of low copper prices, Røros Copper Works simply declared bankruptcy and went out of business.

But Røros remains. The forests have regrown, and the town has reinvented itself as a winter destination for cross-country skiing and snowmobiling, and in the summertime with hiking, and trail biking. Paradoxically, the town now thrives by promoting the very wilderness that it had obliterated in the preceding 300 years.

I went for a hike one afternoon, following a trail that led through the slag heaps to a straggly birch forest on the outskirts of town. I walked up a wild mountain slope along paths marked for use by bikers and cross-country skiers, depending on the season. The resilience of the forest surprised me. Once stripped bare, the land has healed itself. The Southern Sámi people are still here too, as are their reindeer herds. They survived.

It made me think of Røros as a metaphor for humanity: we have so scarred the planet, even the atmosphere, in our wild rush toward industry and the mania for endless growth. But if we just simply *stop in time*, then *with time*, Nature will be able to heal herself.

Chapter 47

To Meet a Musk Ox

I couldn't believe it: there are musk oxen in Norway! I was sure they only existed in the far north of Canada, Alaska and Greenland. But indeed, musk oxen have been successfully reintroduced in the mountains of central Norway. (I say "re-introduced" because musk oxen lived in northern Europe during the last glaciation, until about 9,000 years ago.) After several failed attempts to transplant them to Scandinavia, about 300 musk oxen now roam Dovrefjell-Sunndalsfjella National Park. They have become a huge draw for hikers and wildlife lovers, like myself, who never thought they would have a chance to see a musk ox in the wild.

According to the park website, visitors are "(Almost) guaranteed to see musk oxen: The Musk Ox Trail—a network of paths designed to give you good chances of spotting musk oxen—opened in the summer of 2017.... You can encounter musk oxen along the entire trail."

And so on our route back south to Oslo, I convinced Teresa to detour through Dovre, just south of Trondheim. Teresa does not share my desire for close encounters of the wildlife kind. But she was happy to stay in a nearby hotel for a day while I frolicked in the land of the musk ox.

I think musk oxen are amazing creatures. For starters, they are not actually oxen. They are not related to cattle. They are genetically related to sheep and goats. But supersized. Musk oxen are also survivors from the Pleistocene Ice Age. The rest of the megafauna from that time are extinct. Mammoths, woolly rhinoceroses, cave bears, sabertooth cats—all gone.

How did musk oxen outlast the others? They were able to thrive in the harsh Arctic environment, where few others creatures can live. They have thick, shaggy fur, and can gorge on tundra greenery all summer and then basically eat nothing all winter. There is also their famous "circle the wagons" strategy when confronted with predators: the adults form a ring standing shoulder to shoulder, horns out, keeping the young ones safe inside the circle.

Encountering a musk ox in the wild seems kind of scary. They weigh up to 450 kilos (1,000 pounds) and can also run up to 60 kph (about 35 mph). On entering the park trail, three separate signposts warn hikers in three different languages: "The musk ox is a peaceful vegetarian, but he may attack if you get too close. You will be in great danger then! If you accidentally meet the musk ox in your path, please make a slowly retreat, then take a big curve around it. *For your own safety: Never go closer than 200 meters....*"

I was appropriately fearful as I began my climb up through a birch forest to the Dovrefjell Plateau, where the trees disappear and there's nothing but alpine tundra as far as the eye can see. I expected to find a hulking beast ready to charge behind every tree and boulder. As I reached the rim of the plateau, I ran into a group of about 20 hikers—obviously one

There must be a musk ox here somewhere.

of the guided, musk-ox treks. It was already 2 p.m., and they looked exhausted. They were clearly done for the day, so I asked them if they had any luck. They laughed ruefully and said no. Hmm. My fear took on a different pallor. What if I got musk-ox skunked?

Just a few hundred meters further along the trail, I saw a dark head and two twitching ears appear over the next hill. Holy crap! Was I too close? I crept up, stealthily, my heart pounding.

Nope. On the other side of the rise, several horses grazed on the scrub. Shit.

Climbing further into the plateau, I began imagining I was seeing musk oxen everywhere. How could one tell at a distance the difference between a musk ox and a big rock?

After another kilometer or so, the trail divided. The right path was the main Musk Ox Trail, a shorter path up a nearby mountain top. According to the park website, is where musk oxen are most often spotted. But I assumed that was the way the guided tour must have gone, and so I decided to go the other way, the longer route that followed a wide valley deep into the park.

The path narrowed into an undulating trail that hid the presence of other hikers. I felt all alone on the tundra. But every twenty minutes or so a hiker would pop up, perhaps 50 meters ahead of me. It's proper etiquette in Norway to say "hie-hie" when you meet another trekker on the road. To that greeting, I added a question: "Did you see a musk ox?" They answered me:

"Nye."

"Nye."

"Not today."

And then: "Yes—but a long way up the valley. You go about two kilometers further to a little park cabin, and then about a kilometer beyond that, take the trail to the right, and another kilometer further, we saw four musk oxen high up the hillside.

But, of course, they move a lot. That was hours ago. Who knows where they are now?"

This sighting gave me hope. It kept me going through the next several hikers who all answered "nye." But I had to keep daylight in mind. I had about four hours of sun left. Though it was late August, I was wearing a flannel shirt and my red, down jacket in the afternoon sun. The wind from the north had an Arctic chill in it, and I knew it would get cold when the sun went down.

I found myself cursing the "(almost) guaranteed" musk ox. This was a spectacular walk. I was virtually alone in these wild, high hills. I love this kind of terrain. The tundra makes me feel fully alive. When I die, I hope the last thing I imagine is walking through hills just like these. If I could do that forever, that would be heaven. And yet, here I was, strolling through my absolute perfect version of heaven, squinting at rocks, thinking only of musk oxen.

"I don't need to see no stinkin' ox!" I said out loud. But I knew I was lying. I wanted a musk ox, and would be bitterly disappointed if I didn't see one, no matter how I protested.

I passed the little cabin. There were very few people on the trail now. I walked alone for some time.

"Ya," said a solo woman hiker. "I saw six. About three kilometers from here. After where the path splits, go to the right."

Hope. But damn, three *more* kilometers? It was now 4 p.m. I had walked about seven kilometers. So, I knew I must walk that far back again. I didn't have 20 klicks in me. I walked about ten minutes further, to where I could see the path forking ahead. I sat down to eat my sandwich and some blueberries and contemplated my options. I scanned the mountains one more time.

Well, look at those two tiny black dots, way up high. More musk ox delerium, surely. I chewed my sandwich, then looked again. Had the dots *moved?* Now my attention was riveted. I cursed the fact I had no binoculars, and my iPhone had a lousy camera app that barely zoomed. Yes, they were moving! These were definitely musk oxen. Weren't they? Was being mesmerized by these moving specks what I had come all this way for? Of course, I knew there was no getting close to a musk ox. Even if I could, that would have been a very bad idea. So, yes, I told myself, this is as good as it gets.

A young man wearing a green T-shirt and orange backpack rounded the bend in front of me.

"Hie, hie," I greeted him." I think I see some musk oxen on the slope. Would you like me to show you where?"

His name was Jaime. He was from Switzerland and no stranger to mountains. He said he had also seen several musk oxen further up the valley. So these were bonus oxen as far as he was concerned. He checked out my twin specks, then pulled a camera out from his bag with a proper zoom lens. My eyes widened. Click, click. He gave me the camera, and I pointed it at the two specks. Zoom, zoom. At highest magnification, suddenly I could see their long dark faces, framed by the swooping horns, like a flip-curl sixties hairstyle. Their broad, brown noses pointed straight toward us.

With a jolt I realized that *they* were looking at *us*. I imagined what we looked like to them: a red speck and a green-orange speck, way down in the valley.

I thanked the Swiss, and he said goodbye, leaving me alone with the specks.

I felt a funny sensation, seeing myself as I imagined the musk ox did. I felt their—I struggle for the word—indifference? From their perspective, we humans trudging across their home meant nothing. There was no significance to this moment. Under their gaze, I felt I was dissolving into the tundra. Dis-solve, yes that was the word. I later looked it up, *dissolve* comes from the Latin root that means *to untie*. That was how I felt, untied, unmoored in the moor. Untethered in the tundra. Free of significance.

It was easy, then, to get up and turn around. I looked once more up the slope to the musk oxen, and then to the valley ahead, the river running off far into the never-ending tundra. Some day, I would walk that way, all the way. But not today. The hike back to the car was long and sweet. My step was light, and I felt at ease. There was no one coming out along the trail, as evening was near. Then to my surprise, a man and a woman popped up, walking toward me. Their backpacks were large. It was clear they were carrying camping gear for the night.

"Hie Hie," they said. "Any luck with the musk ox?"

"Yes—but a long way down the valley. You go about two kilometers to a little park cabin, and then about a kilometer beyond that. But, of course—musk oxen move a lot. Who knows where they are now?"

A flâneur, still searching the musk ox, at his heavily musk ox-themed hotel near Dovrefjell.

Chapter 48

When Vikings Built Churches

"King Olaf ruled Norway with a cross in one hand and a sword in the other. Anyone who refused to convert, he beheaded."

I had slipped into a 900-year-old wooden, stave church with a tour group while their Norwegian guide was giving her zealous spiel about the Christianization of Viking lands that took place a thousand years ago, when the sacred places of old gods were burned to the ground and new churches were built for the new religion.

Almost two thousand of these wooden "stave" churches were erected throughout Norway from 1030 to 1350. Only 28 have survived to the present day. While throughout Europe most churches were built out of stone, the Vikings were masters

Left: The Stave Church from Gol, at Norsk Folkemuseum in Oslo. Right: Looking up inside the Gol church, with ribs on the roof like a Viking ship.

at building with wood. Ship-building is what the Vikings knew. So, when it came to building churches, they applied familiar knowledge to an unfamiliar task. For example, they attached swooping dragon heads to the upper gables, exactly like on the prow of a Viking longship, and for the same reason: to protect the crew/congregation from evil influences.

This church (above) from the town of Gol, was dismantled and moved, piece by piece, to the outdoor folk museum in Oslo, where it is the crown jewel of the collection. The museum tour guide continued: "If you look at the wooden ceiling, you can see how it is constructed like the upside-down hull of a ship."

The guide next talked about the mast-like staves. Four eight-meter-high, whole timbers had been turned into giant columns supporting the church's frame. The builders prepped the staves the same way Vikings prepped ship masts. To make the wood impervious to the elements, they lopped all the branches off talls pine and left them standing in the forest for a few years. The trees would swell with sap, seeking to repair their many wounds. The resin in the sap acted like a preservative. The seasoned staves were then cut, and erected on a stone foundation to keep away rot. The rest of the church was built around this frame.

Several hundred years is a long time for wood to last, so almost all stave churches have disappeared. Of the 28 that remain, all but one suffered severe neglect and damage. A few dozen survivors were extensively restored in the late 1800s, and today many of these are recognized as UNESCO World Heritage Sites. The features of these reconstructed churches are modeled after the single church that has maintained its original structure. Built around 1200, the Borgund church, in central Norway, was a place of active worship until 1868. Teresa and I had visited it earlier in our trip:

Borgund Stave Church, the closest-to-original remaining church. Note the dragons on the upper gables.

The black color of the church roof and walls comes from numerous coatings of pitch—a tar-like substance derived from pine resin that the Vikings used to seal their ships and make them watertight. It worked just as well to seal the walls and roofs of their churches.

The Borgund Stave Church also features both Christian and Old Norse iconography, such as snakes and wolves on the exquisitely carved doorways. In some stave churches, there are even heads carved into roof beams that look more like Thor and Odin than any recognizable icons of saints. Clearly, the Vikings were hedging their bets with the new religion by including protective symbols of the old ways.

Teresa adores the stave churches: "On the outside, they look like incredible, ominous, awe-inspiring pieces of art," she told me after one of our several visits. "The dark wood and swooping dragons on the roofs remind me of Thai spirit houses. And then you walk inside, and it's like a warm embrace. The wood interiors feel so cosy and intimate. It must have felt like such a safe place to enter, especially during the cold, northern winters. And the colors they painted on the inside are so exuberant, bursting with color and life. I can imagine what it must have been like to walk through a gray and white winter into a world of luscious blues, golds, and reds...."

These vibrant interior hues were fully restored in the Ringbu Church in a rural community near Lillehammer. It's one of the few stave churches still operating as a church. Here, the staves were painted a mottled blue to look like marble columns. The light from the central chandelier filled the interior and made the wooden beams and ceiling appear to glow.

I could sense the beauty, too, in these churches. Yet they left me feeling conflicted. I felt the clash of symbols: the old religion and the new trying to cohabit the same space. What I admired most about Norwegians of the Viking era was their fierce sense of independence and autonomy. Christianity, back then, was not about repenting one's sins and coming to Jesus. But rather about submitting to a new world order: an order where a national king ruled on behalf of the One True God.

The first Viking to conquer his own people in the name of God was King Harald Bluetooth. He united all of Denmark under his rule (985–86), and briefly conquered Norway. Bluetooth was the first king to grasp how the new religion could legitimize his consolidation of power. Christianity was a useful tool for defeating rebellious earls and chieftains because the new faith required rivals to submit to *God's* authority, and therefore to the *king's* authority, because the king was God's representative on earth. In the twenty-first century, a Danish tech company took Bluetooth's name for their wireless communication devices, as a symbol of the unity their technology could create for their customers.

A decade after Bluetooth, King Olaf Tryggvason (ruled 995–1000 A.D.) used torture and the threat of execution to convert Norwegians to the new faith. Eventually, they revolted. They rose up against Olaf and killed him in battle. A third attempt, by Olaf Haraldsson (ruled 1015–1028) finished the job. "Saint Olaf" as he is remembered, brought back the "sword or cross" conversion policy, and conclusively made Christianity the official religion of Norway in 1020. That date marked the end of the Viking Era.

Today, Norwegians are perhaps the least religious people in the world. While 69% are officially members of the Lutheran Church of Norway, only 2% attend any church at all. This is not hard to explain. Norwegians love their traditions, their culture, and their country. Their national church is a part of that. But on Sunday they prefer to hike, ski, bike, climb, or fish. Their religion has become their great outdoors. That's a faith I'm ready to sign up for.

Part V

Northern Portugal

Peak Flâneur

Chapter 49

Teresa, Queen of the Castle

"Be sure to see the pillory. And the cave behind the castle. You won't find it on your own. Get someone to show you..."

Teresa had not heard her 86-year-old father this excited on the phone in some time. She and I were headed to the village where he was born, in the remote, border town of Penha Garcia in the Portuguese mountains near Spain. José spent the first 10 years of his life there, from 1935–45. Teresa says he remembers swimming in the quarry behind the mountain with his friends: a happy childhood, despite his family's grinding poverty. That ended when he was ten and his parents sent him to Lisbon to work as a delivery boy for a pharmacist. He slept on the pharmacy floor at night, but mostly he recalls the fun he had riding his bike through Lisbon delivering medicines all day, every day.

As a young man, José switched from driving his bike to driving a city bus. He married a young woman from another remote village near his hometown. Like him, Angelina was sent to work when she was ten; in her case, as a child-servant in a rich family's home. Their stories are not unusual for children born during Portugal's Salazar regime. The dictator wanted to keep his country rural and isolated. Like millions of others, José and Angelina wanted a better life for their family—which included a young daughter named Teresa, and so in 1965, they emigrated, first to Canada, then to the USA, where a second daughter, Maggie, was born.

There is actually a monument to emigrants at the entrance to Penha Garcia. The statue shows a young man with a sack of belongings and a hopeful yet scared look on his face. He has no

The monument to emigrants at the entrance to Penha Garcia.

idea what the future holds, but he chooses the unknown—the promise of adventure and a better life. It could well be a statue of José.

When Teresa was a child, her family used to come back to Portugal in the summers, visiting both her mother's and her father's villages. She often told me how beautiful Penha Garcia was, with its castle ruins and the houses built with many-colored local stones. And so, on our drive from France to Lisbon, we decided to stop over for one night. It had been forty years since her last visit.

The village is no longer poor, as attested by the many modern stucco houses among those still made of stone. But it is suffering from the depopulation of the countryside that plagues much of rural Portugal. Many homes are shuttered tight; if not for sale they are outright abandoned. José and his brothers (there were no sisters) all emigrated, and after their parents died, the brothers sold their ancestral home for a paltry 10,000 euros. But the buyer could not afford to renovate, so it is slowly moldering into a state of decay.

Penha Garcia is charming. It is also surprisingly ancient. Archeologists have determined it was settled in the Neolithic, later becoming a Lusitanian fort and then a Roman village. In Medieval times, the castle walls were built to help defend Portugal from Spanish invaders, and then in the fourteenth century, it was turned over to the Knights Templar. Perhaps the repeated threats of violence are why the older houses are clustered so high up the hill, right next to the castle, with the newer ones spread out along the edge of the agricultural valley below.

Teresa and I walked up from our B&B in the lower village to the castle. On the way, we came across the pillory, where lesser criminals were tied by the neck to the stone pillar to be whipped, or perhaps simply exposed to public ridicule and shaming. We still speak of politicians being figuratively "pilloried" by the media when they have done something wrong.

Higher up the hillside we found a tiny museum that housed the collection of antique statues, books and art from the former village priest. "I bet my father remembers him!" Teresa told me. These were exquisite, mostly from the fifteenth century. Sooner or later, some larger museum will come along and claim them as part of Portugal's cultural heritage, but for now this little village proudly displays them for free.

The walk to the castle on the mountaintop was breathtaking — both for the steepness of the climb, and for the beauty of the view.

Much to Teresa's delight, on the back side of the castle we found the hidden cave. To the rear of the over-hang we found an opening into a small tunnel one could crawl through, into the darkness. One *could*, but neither of us opted for that particular

Teresa's photoshoot at the Castelo.

adventure on this particular day. Teresa was convinced her dad must have wriggled inside in the wild and free years of his childhood, before he was sent to the city and put to work.

Down the valley from the cave is the dam and the lake where the quarry used to be. The steep gorge cut through the rock revealed prehistoric fossils from 480 million years ago. A trail called a "Fossil Walk" winds through the valley and back to the village. This was definitely not there in José's time. The valley has been designated part of the UNESCO Geopark Network. Remarkably, this is the *only* Portuguese site in the whole geopark network.

A geopark, a castle, a museum, a monument: Penha Garcia is not without its attractions. It's not a ghost town. But it is not exactly thriving. Teresa asked around to see if anybody remembered her father's family. Only one woman said yes: she remembered the mother-in-law of one of the brothers.

From her childhood, Teresa remembered the village as bustling. There were people living in every home. She said it's sad, now, to see it slowly dying. And yet for her our visit was good. Her memories here are happy ones. She was young and carefree and remembers her paternal grandparents as kind and loving people. Her favorite memory is waking up one morning to have breakfast with her grandmother in the tiny but cozy and immaculate kitchen. Her grandmother asked her if she wanted milk in her coffee, and then stepped outside to milk the goat. Nothing will ever compare to that cup of coffee.

I wonder if perhaps they should build a second monument in Penha Garcia, and the innumerable Portuguese rural villages like it, in honor of the children of all the emigrants who have returned to reconnect with the land of their childhood. They are the ones who fulfilled the hopes of their parents for a better life as strangers in a strange land.

Chapter 50

The Douro Endures

"Twenty years ago, Douro winemakers were harvesting at the end of October. In 2022, we finished the harvest at the end of August. That's climate change, in my lifetime," Nuno told us.

Nuno explained to the four of us visiting his tasting room (me, Teresa, and our dear friends Tom and Paula who joined us for a week), that he and other growers in Portugal's famous Douro River Valley were adapting to the changes as best they could.

The banks of the Douro have been wine-making country at least since Roman times, probably earlier. The roots of the vines grow old and deep, and one may think viniculture in the region will endure forever. The vineyards are so valuable that in 1756 the Douro became the world's first legally-protected wine-growing region. In 2001, the whole valley was designated a UNESCO World Heritage site.

Despite this protection, in the summer of 2022, annual rainfall was *half* the historical average, as all of Portugal went through a catastrophic drought. Those who know anything about wine might opine that a drier clime can only be good for the grapes: an arid climate makes the roots dig deeper, and draws more minerals from the soil into the fruit.

But, according to a 2018 article in *The Porto Protocol*:

Paul Symington, chairman of Symington Family Estates, which owns the Graham's and Cockburn's Port brands, and also produces still Douro wines, points out: "With an apple or a pear, you don't really notice the difference if there's slightly more or less rain. But wine is unbelievably susceptible to minor changes, and we are absolutely a laboratory for climate change."

Climate change is also resulting in dramatic and unprecedented weather events, according to the same article. Sudden downpours flood the steep slopes, washing dry topsoil away forever. Hailstorms, once rare, now strike almost every year.

Villages and vineyards share the banks of the Douro.

Even worse: winter temperatures sometimes turn freakishly warm, causing the grapes to bud prematurely. These have been followed by harsh, killing frosts. What is happening in the Douro shows that climate change is not about a slightly warmer world. It is about unpredictable disruptions and seasonal instability. What once seemed like a river of wine forever suddenly appears frighteningly fragile.

With all this in mind, let's get back to Nuno. Nuno's place was one of three *quintas* Paula, Tom, Teresa and I visited for wine tastings while in the Douro. I was the designated driver. Believe me, on the serpentine roads—really more like donkey tracks covered in cobblestones—that slither up and down the terraced hills of the Douro, you want your DD to be stone-cold sober.

A *quinta* is a Portuguese wine-growing estate. They run the gamut from big corporates like Symington to small growers, like Nuno, with just a small patch of hillside to call their own. We got a good look at many of the *quintas* on our first day when we took a boat ride upriver from the town of Pinhão, a cluster of whitewashed buildings surrounded by vineyards. Despite its compact size, Pinhão is the heart of wine country. Thanks to the train station, it's also the tourist hub of the Douro, where the crowds disperse for bus and boat tours into the hills.

When our boat returned to port, we were hungry, but the restaurants were all full. Finally, we tried the imposing-looking *quinta* of Bomfim on the edge of town, which also served food. This was clearly a fancy place, air-conditioned, with wait staff all wearing matching tan suits. The hostess initially made a face when we told her we had no reservations. Then she smiled, graciously.

"Right now the kitchen is very busy, but if you would kindly wait a little while on the terrace, we will find a place for you. Would you like a port and tonic while you wait?"

They brought us each a glass of white port and tonic on ice with a slice of grapefruit and a sprig of thyme. The concoction proved a revelation. Port is so concentrated and sweet one can only slowly sip a small glass of it. But, diluted in tonic, one gets the whole gamut of white port's subtle flavors—citrus, apricot, honey, vanilla—in a long cool glass that one can slurp rather than sip (and be back in designated-driver mode 90 minutes later). We sat in the sun and drank, watching the wooden tour boats chug up and down the Douro.

The three-course lunch was worthy of my three co-flâneurs, who are lifelong foodies. Only later that afternoon when Teresa googled Bomfim did she breathlessly inform the rest of us that we had stumbled upon the best *quinta* restaurant in the whole Douro, with a Michelin-star celebrity chef, Pedro Lemos.

The next day, we found Nuno Gonzalez's *quinta*, Quinta da Fonte do Milho, just a few kilometers from our guesthouse in the countryside. The experience could not have been more different than Bomfim.

Nuno's place was right by the roadside, and indeed, we almost missed it. There was no fancy building, just a small stone store, surrounded by a vineyard. Nuno greeted us at the entrance and took us out to a vine-covered wooden terrace right at the edge of the vineyard that overlooked the valley. To accompany his wines, he brought us a plate of olives, two kinds of tapenade, olive oil, and almonds—all from his own trees. Plus fresh bread and two flavors of homemade jam (pumpkin and tomato) made from his garden.

Nuno is tall and handsome, with short dark hair and a sunburned face. In his mid-forties, he radiates vitality and a passion for life, especially for his wines and his family vineyard. The vineyard was started by his grandmother in 1933, and then taken over by his father. He told us that as a young man, he had wanted nothing to do with the family business. So he went away and got a job at Volkswagen, eventually rising to become the head of their Portuguese complaints department. After fourteen years, he realized this was not what he wanted to do for the rest of his life.

So Nuno came back to the vineyard, which he now runs. He's made some changes. His father used to sell all their grapes to big companies. Seven years ago, Nuno began making his own wine. Like many other small *quintas*, he and his workers still stomp their own grapes. He only makes 10,000 bottles a year. But his wine sells out. It tastes fantastic, too. Maybe it was the sun and the olives and the homemade jam on the side, but I swear it

Nuno Gonzales, with a bottle of his wine.

tasted as good, if not better, than anything from Bomfim (please don't take my word that it's good; you can order it from his website: www.quintadafontedomilho.pt).

Nuno also made changes in the way his wines are grown, participating in a sustainable growers' network that practices innovations like planting clover in the soil next to the vines, which fixes nitrogen in the soil, reducing the need for artificial fertilizers. This, he explains, is all part of adapting to the challenges of a changing climate. In fact, he has chosen the clover leaf as the emblem for his wine.

You can tell he loves all of it, even the pouring of wine for random visitors at his door, and feeding them enough food for lunch, at no extra cost.

"At Volkswagen, I used to spend all my days listening to unhappy people complain," he told us with a grin. "Now, I get to make people happy, all day long."

Chapter 51

The Exquisite Decrepitude of Old Porto

Porto's old town reminds me of a vintage port wine that's passed its prime. Yes, it's gone a bit musty. But one can still taste how grand it must once have been. Many of the old city's historic buildings seem to have been left standing not so much out of respect for the past, but because nobody ever got around to knocking them down and erecting something new. Aside from some well-kept cathedrals, a few swanky hotels and modern new apartments, most of the old town seems simply to be moldering in place. Oh sure, there is some construction going on here and there. A new subway station has ripped up a main road near the main train station, causing havoc. The renewed market is luminously clean and bustling with bio-wine purveyors and organic produce. But such attempts at modernization barely keep pace with the rate of decay.

As a friend who knows Porto well told us, "The city seems to be held together with string and UNESCO goodwill." Indeed, Porto was designated a UNESCO World Heritage City in 1996, and in 2018 the EU declared the city a leader in heritage conservation. Of course, part of this "conservation" has been good luck. Porto escaped the earthquake that leveled Lisbon in 1755, and avoided the kinds of fires that devastated many ancient European cities.

For flâneurs like Teresa and me (and our friends Tom and Paula who were still with us), the exquisite decrepitude is a big part of Porto's charm. We loved walking the steep streets, surprised round every twisty corner by some architectural relic of a bygone era. Yes, it is sad to see old houses with worn azulejos façades in disrepair, and in many cases abandoned. But

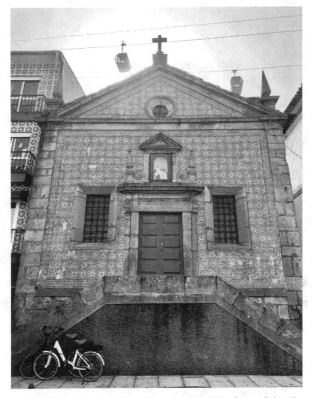

Modern cable cars soar above an old chapel in Porto.

then we see some of them in the midst of being restored, and it's like witnessing a withered rose come back to life.

For example, it's a miracle that the old São Bento Train Station has survived unscathed. Its walls are masterpieces of azulejos paintings—22,000 tiles in all! The grand scenes depict rural life at the turn of the nineteenth century as well as vast panoramas from Portugal's history. This kind of profusion of decorative art is what one normally finds in Portugal's palaces and cathedrals. To find this quality of art in a public station for common travelers is really uplifting. Though the scenes are grand and sweeping, the faces of some individuals—whether

Left: azulejos art on the walls of São Bento Station. Right: the São Bento Station's panoramas feature amazingly expressive individual faces.

kings' or country girls'—are vividly expressive. It seems as if the artist was drawing each one from real life.

One of my favorite discoveries was at the top corners of the old shopping street, Rua da Santa Catarina, where two exuberant Art Nouveau storefronts face each other. The one on the left features the golden head of a beautiful woman. The one on the right features the copper bust of a man, now green with age. His head is turned so that he is staring straight at her: a poignant and very Portuguese-like portrayal of unrequited love that has lasted more than a century.

In some cases, the restoration and repurposing of old buildings are jarring. We came across a McDonald's restaurant in an old Art Nouveau building with a magnificent wrought-iron eagle above the door. Stained glass artwork on the back wall. Crystal chandeliers on the ceiling. A white bas-relief sculpture of naked women dancing on one side. All this above tables full of tourists, scarfing Big Macs.

But then, we also found an old Neo-Gothic bookstore, built in 1906. Livraria Lello has become so famous over time that you have to purchase a ticket in advance just to get inside. And why has this store become famous? Not simply because of the winding wooden double staircase that leads to the upper floor, nor the aura of musty mystery the whole shop exudes. It's because it is one of the places in Porto that inspired J.K. Rowling while she was living here in the early 1990s, writing the adventures of Harry Potter. Apparently, Rowling browsed Livraria Lello regularly, and it became the inspiration both for Hogwart's library and the wizards' Flourish and Blotts Bookshop. For those who read and enjoyed the series, as have I, the crumbling yet magic-infused features of Harry Potter's world capture exactly the sense one gets wandering around the worn yet entrancing streets of old Porto.

I wonder what the future will hold for this ancient city? Construction cranes tower over the landscape now, like strange mechanistic predators. As with Lisbon, real estate values are going up here, and it might price residents out of the city center, already crammed with tourists. When refurbishing takes place, as often as not it is to create short-term rentals instead of new homes. But there are also many signs that the city knows it's the historic beauty that draws the crowds. Old façades are kept, even as the structures behind them are gutted and rebuilt from the ground up.

Overall, I feel hopeful for Porto, this magic-inspiring, glamorous wreck of a town. I pray she finds her way forward with some unique compromise between old and new, culture and progress, history and destiny.

Chapter 52

Who Is Viana do Castelo?

Flâneur Lesson #15: Don't believe the brochure

Viana do Castelo ("Viana of the Castle") is an hour's drive north of Porto, at the mouth of the Lima River. The most prominent feature of this pretty little city is the mountain that juts up, overlooking the harbor and the surrounding land. Much more than a photo op, Monte de Santa Luzia has been a strategic lookout and safe haven since before Roman times. In fact, it is one of the oldest inhabited places in Portugal, dating back 7,000 years to the Mesolithic era.

Teresa and I stayed on this mountaintop in a beautiful old *Belle Epoque* mansion converted into a hotel. In front of us, enhancing the view, is a twentieth-century basilica that looks as if it dropped straight from heaven. It's dome glows gold in the setting sun. Behind us are the ruins of an Iron Age Celtic fort town. I imagine for some readers this will not compute. Aren't the Celts Irish and Scottish? Well, yes, but they came to the British Isles from somewhere, didn't they? There are Celtic ruins in Brittany, Northwest France, as well as Galicia in Northwest Spain and Portugal. If you need any more proof, look to the bagpipes—which you can find in Brittany, Galicia, and, yes, in northern Portugal.

The Iron Age Celts in Portugal intermarried with earlier inhabitants and became the Lusitanians: a loose collection of tribes that modern Portuguese claim as their ancestors. It was very cool to wander the old Celtic ruins on Monte de Santa Luzia and see how these early Portuguese once lived. Their houses are round, grouped together in clusters that were apparently family compounds. The excavated portion is only about one-third of the original settlement, which must have been home to a thousand or more people, living safe and secure, high on the hill, behind the thick stone wall of their citadel.

Safe—until the Romans came and conquered the land, claiming Lusitania as a province of the Empire. There are square buildings plunked in the middle of the fort town of clearly Roman design. Romans occupied the town from around 300 B.C. When the Romans finally left, other waves of invaders

Santa Luzia Basilica

followed: Carthaginians, Suevi, Visigoths, Moors, Galicians. It took until the twelfth century for Alphonso I, the first king of Portugal, to claw back Portugal from the last of the invaders and reestablish an independent kingdom.

In the mid-1200s, the village of Viana was already an important hub for the new nation of Portugal. Viana was an international port, trading wine, fruit and salt with northern Europe in exchange for preserved cod (still a mainstay of the Portuguese diet). Monte de Santa Luzia's strategic mountain defences enabled the town to fend off pirates and thrive. Viana became so vital to the young kingdom of Portugal that the king granted it a city charter in 1258, and the town prospered through the centuries.

A statue of Viana erected in the old town in 1774 depicts Viana as "Queen of the Sea," so the nearby plaque contends. She holds a scepter in one hand (now missing), a ship in the other, and wears a headdress in the shape of a castle. Busts on the four corners indicate the four cardinal directions and the four

Eighteenth-century statue of Viana do Castelo cradling a ship.

continents which brought wealth and abundance to Viana from all around the world.

What's strange about this is that to my knowledge, no other town in Portugal is personified as a woman. Viana is not even a Portuguese woman's name. So I wondered where it came from. The only local story I could find was that once upon a time there was a beautiful but shy princess named Ana who lived in a tower on the hill. A young man was in love with her, but because she was so shy he rarely saw her. Whenever he did, he would tell everyone: "I saw Ana!" — "Vi Ana!" This seemed one of the lamest origin stories I had ever heard.

I did some Internet flâneuring down various rabbit holes (I will not call it *flânoogling*!) and discovered a Celtic-Lusitanian Goddess, *Nabia*, who was "Goddess of waters, fountains and rivers." In Galicia and Portugal still today, numerous rivers bear her name. There is even an ancient fountain in northern Portugal dedicated to the Goddess Nabia. So perhaps **Via**n*a* is an inversion of *Na***via**?

During my search, I discovered and contacted a Portuguese goddess priestess and scholar, Luiza Frazão (www.luizafrazao. com), who has written a book about the Goddess in Portugal. I asked her about Viana, and she wrote back to me:

Dear Tim, In which concerns the statue, she looks like Brigântia, goddess of civilization, of the city, with the tower as a headdress, and the boat... she was the goddess of maritime activities also. But mind that this statue is from the XVIII century... anyway it could be manifesting a very ancient memory. Brigântia was very important here, Bragança and Braga towns are called after her....

Brigantī, according to Wikipedia means "The High One." The name is derived from the Proto-Indo-European root of *berg* ("to rise"). *Berg,* of course, means an ancient medieval fortress or town—a castelo—which we find in modern times in city names like Strasburg and Pittsburg.

Whether Brigânti or Navia, when the Romans arrived and set up residence in the hill fort, they might simply have changed the name of the castelo's Lusitanian Goddess to one they were more familiar with. Perhaps *Viana* is a version of *Diana,* a Goddess the Romans also called *Lucina,* for she was goddess of the cycles of the moon, and hence all things to do with women's cycles and childbirth. Lucina found her way into Catholicism as patron saint of childbirth—St. Lucia. *Santa Luzia,* in Portugeuse. As in *Monte de Santa Luzia.*

Traje a Vianesa - c. 1880s

My photo from the Viana do Castelo costume museum.

In modern times, Viana do Castelo has dwindled from its glory days. Except for one brilliant light: The annual *Festa da Senhora da Agonia* (Festival of Our Lady of Agony), renowned throughout Portugal and the world. The heart of this festival are processions of hundreds of local *Lavradeira* (women farmers) from the surrounding inland villages, adorned in traditional embroidered dresses and bedecked with gold jewelry.

Although we missed the festival by two months, the town has a festival-costume museum containing preserved costumes. Traditionally, each rural village had its own distinct embroidered costumes that the women farmers wore to their festivals. The museum lays out the evolution of the patterns and colors through the years, including stunning photographs that go as far back as the mid-1800s.

The online tourist guides rather glibly date the origins of the festival to the declaration of a Catholic feast day in 1744 to the Virgin Mary as "Our Lady of Sorrows." The purpose of the women's procession is so that by their prayers, Mary will calm the seas and protect their men when they are off fishing. The website Visitportugal.com describes the procession to the sea like this: "The image of Nossa Senhora da Agonia, dressed in her blue and purple cloak, is carried aboard a trawler, amidst fireworks and the ringing of bells, so that she can bless the sea and thereby make it calm and forever generous in the sustenance that it provides."

As by now you can imagine, I suspected there was another story beneath the surface. The costumes are worn by *lavradeira* — women farmers, from villages in the fertile inland hills. *Not* fishermen's wives and daughters. The museum also says women traditionally did all the work on the farms, from plowing to sowing. They were the mainstay of the economy, not dependent on their men for survival. The museum's story is that the origins of these festivals are not known.

I suspected the Catholic Church might have taken over an older pre-Christian summer festival and Christianized it (as the Church has done with Christmas, Easter and Carnivale). 1744 is a long way back; so there's not much hope of finding evidence of such a reinvention. But in my search, I came upon a Portuguese Master's thesis by João Vasconcelos on the politics of folk culture that painstakingly documents how 100 years ago Catholic priests in northern Portugal *deplored* the summer festivals for their "pagan" elements.

According to Vasconcelos' sources, from the 1930s–1950s, during the Salazar dictatorship, the Church took firm control of the summer festivals and *reinvented* them as Christian processions with Mary firmly planted at the center of things. The aim, according to one priest quoted in the thesis, was to keep the villagers so busy with sanctioned activities during the festival, they would have no spare time to sin.

As I looked out from my hotel balcony at the distant Lima River, with Viana do Castelo spread out far below, and the Santa Luzia Basilica roof glowing in the fading light of the sun, I could not help but wonder what other ancient secrets might lie buried beneath the church's foundations—foundations built upon a Lusitanian *berg*.

For me, one of the blessings of flâneuring is to have the time to pause and reflect when a certain story does not quite ring true. To question, dig a little deeper and perhaps uncover different narratives. It is not just about observing the surface of things. It's about wandering the poorly-lit byways of the past, rather than sticking to the main streets of history—no matter how well presented in a church record or tourist brochure.

Chapter 53

Portugal's Green Coast

Portugal is famous for its light, fruity, effervescent and affordable wine called *vinho verde*—literally, "green wine." I've been a fan for decades, even before I married a Portuguese wife. You can get it almost anywhere: in the US, Canada, France, and even Norway, as Teresa and I discovered this past summer. *Vinho verde* comes in white, red and rosé varieties, but what you cannot get is *vinho verde* that is green. It's called *green* wine because it's bottled young. You don't store it in a cellar, you drink it right away.

So I know my *verde*, or so I thought. What I did not know is that *vinho verde* comes only from *Costa Verde*, Portugal's "Green Coast." The region runs north from the Douro to the Spanish border, and inland to the Serra do Barroso—the mountain range that divides north Portugal down the middle.

While most of Portugal has an arid climate, the Costa Verde is downright lush. It gets more rainfall than any other part of the country. Atlantic breezes and inland hills also moderate the temperature, so it's not too warm in summer, not too cold in winter. This is Portugal's Goldilocks territory. It's no surprise that people have lived here since prehistoric times.

We drove up the Atlantic road from Porto, passing ancient pine forests, wild sand dunes, and unspoiled beaches with just the occasional resort village interrupting the green coast. After a few days in the charming town of Viana do Castelo, we continued to the mouth of the Minho River which forms the northern border with Spain.

Driving north, we saw many hikers walking along the roadside. They were pilgrims headed for Santiago on one of the

Ponte de Lima

Portuguese routes of the Camino Trail. At the border town of Valença we turned south and traveled through the forested hills and *vinho verde* vineyards to Ponte de Lima, an ancient, pre-Roman City with an intact Roman bridge, all of it fringed with green.

Before the bridge was built, a conquering Roman army once famously refused to cross this river. A rumor had spread among the troops that the Lima was actually the River Lethe—the mythical river of forgetfulness that washes away the memory of whoever enters it. Finally, their general, Decius Juno Brutus, spurred his horse across the waters. On reaching the far bank, he turned and called to each of his men by name, thus reassuring them he had not lost his memory, and neither would they. To commemorate this unforgettable tale, an ersatz phalanx of Roman soldiers now stands on one side of the river, while a statue of the general on horseback beckons them on the far side.

South of Ponte de Lima, near the town of Braga, a detour up a winding mountain road took us to Citânia de Briteiros, probably the largest Iron Age settlement in Portugal. Some 20,000 Lusitanians lived on this sprawling hilltop in the centuries before and after the Roman conquest. Surrounded by forest, the stone foundations of the houses and walls of this once powerful fort-city are now moss-covered and silent.

The Lusitanians fought tenaciously against the Empire in a war that raged for 16 years. The historian Stabo called it "the Fiery War." In the end, the Lusitanians succumbed. But their fight for freedom became an enduring symbol of Portuguese nationalism; it would take more than a thousand years for the nation to become independent again.

The rebirth of the nation happened here in Costa Verde, in the city of Guimarães, just south of Briteiros, known today as the "Cradle of Portugal." Teresa and I stayed there for three days, where we learned how the founding of her country unfolded in three easy steps:

Step 1: A.D. 868. The Christian kingdoms of northern Iberia defeat the Moors, pushing them south of the Douro River. The military leader of the Christian forces, Vímara Peres, becomes the first count and governor of the newly liberated Galician province, Portucale. He makes his seat of government in a town that will be named *Vímara* in his honor. Through "phonetic evolution," the pronunciation of "Vímara" morphs in a few hundred years into "Guimarães."

Step 2: A.D. 1096. Two hundred years later, the Christian kings of northern Iberia are not happy with the slow progress of the war against the Moors. They appoint as governor of Portucale a young nobleman, Count D. Henrique of Burgundy, who was married to Teresa, the daughter of the king of Burgundy. From their base in Guimarães, the young power couple try to establish Portucale as an independent kingdom. But Henrique dies before they accomplish their plan.

Step 3: A.D. 1128. The son of Henrique and Teresa, Alfonso Henriques, eventually succeeds in establishing the kingdom of Portugal—fighting against the Moors in the south, the rival

Christian kings in the north, and his fiercest opponent of all, Teresa, his *mother* (who changed her mind about an independent Portugal). The bitter family feud culminates in the Battle of São Mamede, fought in the streets of Guimarães in 1128. The battle is remembered as the birth pangs of Portugal. When Alfonso Henriques wins, he declares himself king of independent Portugal in 1139. As Alfonso I, he eventually gains Portugal's legal recognition from the neighboring kingdoms. Alfonso I goes on to lead his troops south, and with the help of Crusaders from northern Europe, in 1147 he reclaims Lisbon from the Moors, effectively doubling the size of his new nation.

We stayed at Guimarães in the Monastery of Santa Marinha da Costa, which in modern times has been turned into a hotel. It was constructed in the tenth century by the order of Countess Mumadona Dias. Her story is just as crucial to the history of Guimarães as any of the men who fought the battles and won the wars. Countess Dias governed Portucales jointly with her husband, Count Hermenegildo González. After he died, she held sole authority until her own death in 950. She initiated and paid for the construction of the Castle of Guimarães, for the purpose of protecting the monastery and the people from both Moors and Viking raiders. The town of Guimarães developed in the corridor between these two buildings, and the castle eventually became the headquarters of the court of the counts of Portucale.

The monastery has been rebuilt several times over the centuries. Even so, it was thrilling to walk through the vast empty halls, and to walk upon Portugal's foundation stones — even if only metaphorically so. Teresa tells me that apparently young Alfonso Henriques, who became a knight at age 16, used to ride through the halls of the monastery on horseback! I was not able to find an online source to substantiate this — as if I trust *Wikipedia* more than Teresa! But I love the thought of Alfonso

Henriques galloping up and down, creating havoc among the monks. Little did they suspect the role this fiery young man would play in the birth of the nation.

Behind the monks' quarters is a garden and a large wilderness park. I took a walk there one afternoon. The park is quiet, overgrown with tall trees and vines, with just a few leaf-covered paths through the woods. Bits of worked stone push through the foliage here and there, as a reminder this hillside, like that of Briteiros, was inhabited since before the Bronze Age, and that beneath Costa Verde's greenery, so much of Portugal's past lies still, waiting to be discovered. A *vinho verde* vineyard grows right up against the side of the park. I imagined those deep roots sucking up particles of those old stones along with the moisture, infusing the grapes, and the young wine, with the flavor of Portugal's history.

Chapter 54

Behind the Mountains

The northeast corner of Portugal is called *Trás-os-Montes*, which translates as "Behind the Mountains." It's the one part of her country that Teresa has never been to. So it was high on our must-see list for our trip through the north of her native land. "Behind the Mountains" conjures up a region remote and forgotten. Indeed, it is one of the most sparsely populated areas of the country, and one of the poorest. Teresa tells me the people from the region describe their climate as, "nine months of winter, and three months of hell."

Driving into *Trás-os-Montes*, the road rises through steep rough hills—slopes too precipitous for even olive trees to grow. The land is green, but not the verdant green of the *Costa Verde* region to the west. It's a dry, dusty green: pine trees and scrub bushes. In places, the land was blackened as if afflicted by some Mordor-like curse. The metaphor is not far off the mark: the intense heat of hotter-than-average summers has caused forest fires in recent years, charring and scarring the countryside.

Villages on the other side of the mountains seemed run-down and empty. Though clearly, they were not. There were cars parked on the roadsides. But depopulation is a major problem for the region. We saw the occasional pensioner out for a stroll or donkey cart on the road. But many buildings seemed closed up, with more than the usual number of them abandoned and falling apart. Between villages, we saw more goats than people.

In some ways, the neglect this forgotten region has suffered has been a blessing. Lack of attention and investment has left it poor, which has led to a kind of stoic self-reliance. People depend on what they grow, and it turns out they can grow a lot. The region is Portugal's main producer of chestnuts; it also grows walnuts, almonds, cherries, persimmons, and grapes, of course, and its olive oil is said to be the best in the country. There's also lots of meat because so much of the land is only good for grazing: sheep, goats, pigs, and the region's own unique breed of cattle. Plus wild game, which shows up on many menus: boar, deer, pheasant, partridge, rabbit. In short, *Trás-os-Montes* is very much a microcosm of an older, wilder Europe. People may be poor, but they don't go hungry.

Of course, isolation and self-sufficiency are no longer a defence against the forces of modernity. In February 2022 the Portuguese government approved plans to build open-pit lithium mines in several sites across the country, including *Trás-os-Montes*. Portugal has an estimated 60,000 tons of the new "white gold," which is needed to power electric vehicles and other devices essential for Europe's transition to a post-carbon economy. No surprise, people living in the places targeted for the mines object. Even if jobs are provided, in one generation a mine would destroy *forever* farms that have lasted millennia. But does anyone in the capital really care? Isn't it all an empty wasteland "behind the mountains"?

Arriving in Bragança, the region's capital, Teresa and I were blissfully unaware of this yet-to-be-fought battle of the mines. The heart of the town is a Medieval fortress surrounded by a high stone wall. Tourists do not seem to have invaded; the streets of the old town are filled with local shops and people going about their daily lives. The place seemed downright serene. On the outskirts of the town there are a few patches of cropland. Beyond, a vast northern plateau stretches all the way to the border with Spain. This area is the 75,000-hectare Monteshino National Park, one of the largest in Portugal. It's a wildlife refuge, that includes some 90 villages, but a total population of no more than 9,000 people.

Festival masks from Trás-os-Montes

Due to their isolation, these tiny villages, as well as many others in *Trás-os-Montes,* have retained some of their old, pre-Christian ways better than most other parts of the country, especially their annual winter festivals, which feature bizarrely masked and costumed figures that parade through the streets, dancing and sometimes whacking people with their staffs. A costume museum in Bragança contains three whole floors of these costumes, which vary from village to village.

In Italy I had encountered the mysterious figure of the "Wild Man" in paintings, statues and legends. I knew he was also at the center of many "pagan" festivals in the more isolated regions of Europe, from Norway to Greece, so it was not surprising to see these variations in remote, northern Portugal. In fact, it was rather like bumping into an old friend. I felt so at home with these costumed mannequins. Some were shaggy beasts with horns. Others were so stylized they seemed almost Japanese.

I loved the idea that festivals and traditions can encode the past for thousands of years, long before anyone was writing "history." Of course, this is not something one can ever prove, say, with C-14 dating techniques. I remember, though, attending a festival on the remote Greek island of Skyros twenty years ago. In the evenings I watched masked men in hairy costumes race through the steep and narrow streets and dance till dawn, with fifty pounds of cowbells tied around their waists. In the daytime, I managed to interview some of these dancers. One burly Greek told me, "You don't just dress up as the *Geros*. You become *possessed* by his spirit. That is what gives you the strength to run all night long, with the bells."

To look at these festivals as cultural artifacts of the past is, I think to miss the very thing that enables them to survive. There's an intangible living spirit in a "forgotten" land like *Trás-os-Montes*—a spirit that *does not forget*. Instead, it passes something of itself along, generation after generation, through the people that continue to make the land their home, and follow its ways.

Chapter 55

Griffon Vultures and Top-Hat Little Boy Jesus

Massive dark wings covered the sun. We looked up. About a dozen giant vultures glided overhead, so low we could see their scrawny necks and bald heads looking for food. Were they checking us out as we stood by the side of the car, desperately punching our Apple map app? Did they intuit that we were lost? They whirled in patient circles.

Teresa and I were not stranded in some Arizona desert. We were on the outskirts of Miranda do Douro, the second-largest town in *Trás-os-Montes*. The town is frequented by three species of giant carrion eaters: Griffon, Black, and the rare Egyptian vulture. We had just arrived and here they were, like some Wild-Kingdom welcome wagon. Finding us, sadly, not about to die, the vultures flapped away towards the Douro River.

Yes, this is the same Douro River renowned for its beautiful terraced vineyards. But Miranda do Douro is about 150 kilometers upstream from the chi-chi port quintas with their tasting rooms and tourist spas. Here, the Douro snakes through wild mountains, forming the northeastern border between Portugal and Spain. The river splits the two nations apart as it winds its way around Miranda do Douro, creating a chasm so spectacular and deep that it is known as Portugal's Grand Canyon. In this granite gorge the vultures build their nests and ride the strong winds that blow between the cliffs.

During our brief two days in Miranda do Douro we saw these massive birds of prey everywhere. They own the skies above the town. I suppose the local people are so used to them, they don't even notice when shadows cross the sun. The wingspans of the largest vultures are eight feet across. They are social birds too, swooping and riding the thermals in groups of four to twelve. The ones we saw were mostly griffon vultures—easily identified from below by the five feathers at the end of each wingtip that look like fingers.

The birds are a suitable symbol for Miranda do Douro, a border outpost that seems to have been left to its own devices. Founded in Medieval times, its high towers and thick stone walls were once bulwarks against Spanish incursions.

In the sixteenth century, Miranda do Douro was elevated to the region's political, military and spiritual capital, with a bishop in residence in his own palace. That all changed in 1762 when the Spanish invaded in force. Their cannons bombed the castle to smithereens. One third of the townspeople died in the attack. Those survivors who had means—the political leaders, the wealthy, the *bishop*—left for Bragança, which became the new capital of *Trás-os-Montes*. Only those too poor to evacuate stayed to rebuild: peasants, artisans, workers.

Miranda do Douro never recovered its past glory. The wrecked castle and broken walls are part of the town's heritage now, and the Medieval old town looks like not much has changed in the past few hundred years. Very few tourists make it this far into the wilderness, and the town's isolation has helped to preserve much of its authentic charm.

Although the population of Miranda do Douro is still much smaller than it was a few hundred years ago, today there is a new town center with two streets of shops and banks and restaurants, and a small suburb of modern houses overlooking the canyon. Pretty clearly the gorgeous view is drawing some retirees to the area. Overall, the town seems prosperous while still retaining its original soul.

Miranda do Douro has preserved its unique festivals, costumes, dances, and traditional embroidery—including the ornate patterns on the dramatic hooded winter coat that has become an icon of the town. One finds it on display in shops and museums, and even on a statue in the center of town. It is the sort of coat one would expect a hero from *The Lord of the Rings* to wear when riding through a storm—perhaps Aragorn traveling in disguise. The town has even retained its own unique dialect, *Mirandês*, an official language of Portugal spoken by only 10,000 people in the district.

Perhaps most fascinating of all, Miranda do Douro has its very own legend of a visitation of Jesus Christ. He appeared during the fateful 1762 battle with the Spanish, so the story goes, as a boy wearing a top hat and brandishing a sword. The divine lad was seen by many people leading the charge. He gave courage to the Portuguese to fight on. Yes, they lost the battle. But the memory of that blessed visitation lives on in Miranda do Douro, concretized in a statue of Top-Hat Little Boy Jesus in the town cathedral.

If you think it odd that Top Hat Little Boy Jesus did not help the town *win* against the Spanish, then you have not grasped something essential about the Portuguese that I think I have begun to understand. Top Hat Little Boy Jesus came to sanctify their defeat: to turn the desolation of loss into a spiritual blessing.

Preserved in a glass case, this porcelain Jesus seems no more than a toddler. Several outfits hang on either side of him. He is dressed in different costumes for different festive occasions throughout the year, including a military uniform, as a memory of that fateful battle that destroyed the town and yet gave the survivors an enduring reminder that they had not been forgotten, at least not by Top Hat Little Boy Jesus.

I took a hike along the bank of the gorge one day, accompanied, of course, by vultures that glided above me in graceful circles—hopeful, perhaps, that I might stumble, slip, and tumble down the slope to a happy ending (for them). Once

Left: Miranda do Douro's famous cloak. Right: Top Hat Jesus.

more I proved a disappointment. On the walk I found small farms growing an incredible diversity of crops, everything from persimmon trees to chestnuts, almonds, and oak orchards. Why would anyone cultivate *oaks*? Because the pigs who provide the region's famous flavorful ham grow fat on a diet of acorns.

On the walk I met an old sheep farmer out with his flock. He greeted me, I suppose, in Mirandese, then switched to Portuguese. When I said, hopefully, "English?" he shook his head and countered, "Español?" "Italianio?" He spoke four languages to my one-and-a-quarter, but we had none in common.

Undeterred, he ascertained that I was not, in fact, lost, just out for a ramble. He offered directions to a great viewpoint he knew, a few kilometers down the road. How very Portuguese, to want to help a stranger, even if he's just a flâneur. With some chagrin, I later realized this polyglot farmer had dark hair, and probably he saw *me* as the old man in this encounter!

Perhaps the most hopeful conversation Teresa and I had in town was with a young couple who worked at a local café. They told us they both grew up in Miranda do Douro. I asked, why did you decide to stay when so many young people leave the rural areas for the cities? Well, they replied, it's only a few hours by bus to Porto, so if you want to visit the city, now it's easy. But it is much less expensive to live here, even on minimum wage. And—they looked at each other—life is good here.

The young woman served us a robust and delicious local red wine with our meal, grown, fermented and bottled right here in Miranda do Douro. Its logo is the griffon vulture. We bought a bottle to take with us, to help keep alive the memory of those omnipresent, five-fingered black wings, forever circling above this ancient town.

Miranda do Douro's famous griffon vultures.

Chapter 56

Postcards from the Paleolithic

What might it be like to get a postcard from the deep past? How about 5,000 postcards from as far back as 22,000 years ago? This is what archeologists discovered during the early 1990s in Portugal's remote Coa Valley in the Alto Douro, near the border with Spain. The valley was just south of Trás-os-Montes, so Teresa and I decided to drop by the Coa Valley Archeological Park, and check out their new museum.

An early UNESCO report on the park described it as "the biggest open-air site of paleolithic art in Europe, if not in the world." Usually, we think of paleolithic art as cave paintings.

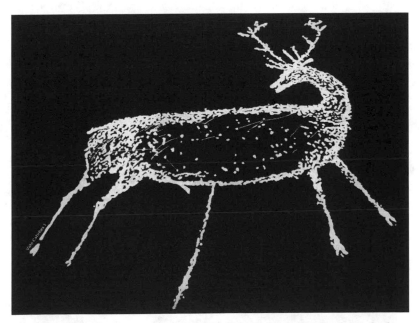

Palaeolithic art from the Coa Valley Archeological Park (my photo from the museum).

The Coa drawings are out in the open, spread over 23 sites along the Coa and Douro River valleys. Also, the drawings are not painted, they are line drawings carved directly into the stone, which is why they survived the elements for millennia. That, plus the fact that this is a remote and uninhabited borderland. It is so wild that an Iberian wolf-restoration program is also underway in the Coa Valley region.

The art may be prehistoric but it is not primitive. These artists had *talent*. They brought to life the animals crucial to our early ancestors' survival—deer, horses, wild goats, aurochs (large prehistoric cattle)—and also human figures. These provide an amazing glimpse of how prehistoric people saw their world and themselves. UNESCO says of these World Heritage Site drawings:

> Dating from the Upper Palaeolithic to the final Magdalenian/ Epipalaeolithic (22.000–8.000 BCE), [the drawings] represent a unique example of the first manifestations of human symbolic creation and of the beginnings of cultural development…. The rock art… *throws an exceptionally illuminating light on the social, economic, and spiritual life of our early ancestors* [italics mine].

Teresa and I first heard about the Coa Valley Archeological Park during a previous trip to Portugal in 2003. This was my first visit to her native land. At the time I was writing a book on the religions of pre-Christian Europe, so visiting Coa was at the top of my list. I don't remember much at all from that trip. But I sure remember Coa, for all the wrong reasons.

The park then was less than a decade old. At that time there was no museum. One booked a guided tour in a jeep to visit the rock art on-site. Our jeep careened through crazy-steep dirt roads with hairpin turns and no shoulder at all. Just an extra inch or two of dirt and a sheer drop. The road was rocky, muddy, and rutted, and I remember being thrown from side to side in my seat. We feared for our lives sometimes as the jeep slipped on a curve or slithered through the mud.

It seemed to take hours just to get to the first art-rock site, which was... unsatisfying. What we didn't realize was that the same flat stone surfaces had been used time and again by different artists through the centuries. They etched new figures right on top of the old ones. Individually, the drawings may have been masterpieces, but all we saw were jumbles of squiggles. Our guide would trace out the lines of some of the specific animals. But even with his help, it was hard to make out anything clearly. This went on site after site, until finally, exhausted, frustrated and defeated, we just wanted to go back to our hotel. Our photos of the day were terrible.

So in 2022, Teresa and I were quite clear: we wanted to experience the new museum, but *not* the slog through the enormous park. We did learn in advance that the museum, which opened in 2010, does not contain any of the *original* art. That's all still in the valley (and can still only be accessed via a guided jeep tour). However, the museum website promised state-of-the-art technical innovations in bringing the prehistoric drawings to life. Bingo.

The outside of the museum is a long concrete wedge in the hillside overlooking the wild river valley. The underground entrance looks as if it leads to a bunker or a bomb shelter. Inside, everything is dim, but the displays light up with neon colors that shimmer and glow green, red, purple and blue as the story of the paleolithic drawings unfolds. The absolute best thing about the museum is that it isolates the individual drawings that overlap on the rocks so that you can see each of their outlines clearly. Sometimes the outlines are projected right onto replicas of the original rocks so that the art seems to pop right out. In one case, they even animate some of the figures: you see the etched outline of an ibex and then it springs to life, jumping and prancing across the rock as if frolicking on a cliffside.

The museum also highlighted some of the artistry involved. In several cases, there were animals that appeared to have two heads—but were in fact one animal with its head turned first in one direction and then in another, as if to portray the animal in motion—an artistic technique once thought to have been invented by that Cubist late-comer, Picasso!

The rare human figures from the Paleolithic period are mysterious and strange. The face on one figure looks absolutely as if Picasso drew it (below). Two other figures are so explicitly phallic one has to wonder if this is evidence that men have been

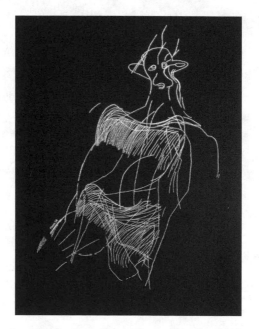

Clearly Picasso stole everything from the Stone Age (my photo from the museum).

exaggerating their manhood since prehistoric times. Or, perhaps, more poetically, one could assume the artists were making symbolic connections between big penises and fecundity? Personally, I'm sticking with the exaggeration hypothesis.

As the museum notes explain, even after the Paleolithic era, people kept drawing art on the rocks in these valleys. There's a wealth of etchings dating from the Iron Age, the time of the Lusitanians. Some are on horseback, or depicted bearing a spear and round shield, which is exactly how the Roman writer Strabo described Lusitanian warriors.

There are even drawings from Medieval times. These latecomers also discovered the Coa Valley, and added their own

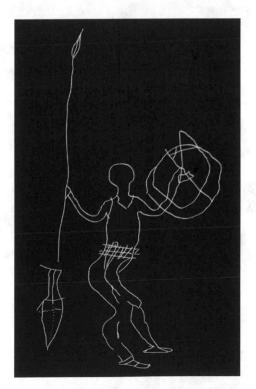

Iron Age Lusitanian (my photo from the museum).

works of art. It made me a little sad that this incredible lithic canvas had been lost to humanity for over a thousand years, and that in modern times, we would not be adding to this rock tapestry for our descendants yet to come. A few thousand years into the future, as humanity wanes and perhaps may wax again, wouldn't it be great to have our story told, alongside these others, on the rocks of Coa Valley?

There is one final element to this story I only discovered while writing about our visit and gathering information online. Neither Teresa nor I realized that when the Coa Valley drawings were first discovered in the early 1990s, they were at the center of a massive political controversy: a conflict of values and priorities that drew international attention to the nation, and may have contributed to bringing down Portugal's government at the time.

Those archeologists who discovered the drawings were actually working at the behest of the national energy company, EDF. The plan was to build a dam in the Coa River, and the archeological survey was just a required box to tick. The discovery of ancient rock carvings came as a most unwelcome shock. For awhile, EDF even attempted to disprove the ancient age of the drawings and press ahead with the dam.

The archeologists called UNESCO, which quickly produced an initial report attesting to the antiquity and value of the art. Other archeologists began additional investigations in the Coa Valley region and discovered even more rock drawings. A Portuguese citizens group in defense of the Coa arose with a slogan, *As gravuras não sabem nadar* ("The carvings don't know how to swim"). The government vowed to proceed with the dam. Both national and international media heaped scorn upon them. A national groundswell against the dam arose and in the 1995 elections the government was defeated and the dam project was canceled. But for that dramatic result, the prehistoric postcards of the Coa Valley would have remained undelivered, its amazing, multilayered world of animals and humans buried forever in sediment and silt.

When Teresa and I finally emerged back from the museum, blinking, into the light, we felt transformed by the whole experience, and in awe of the amazing human beings who not only made this harsh landscape their home so many thousands of years ago, but sent postcards to us in the future.

Chapter 57

Peak Flâneur

We have been flâneuring for a year now. Teresa and I left the US in October 2021 and except for five weeks back in Maryland, we have been living and traveling in Europe for the past 12 months. We had much to learn about what it is to be twenty-first-century "Mature Flâneurs." Not just learning, but also embellishing and enriching the nineteenth-century concept.

We brazenly turned the noun into a verb and *flâneured* through France, Italy, Spain, Norway, and Portugal. Along the way we invented new terms that did not exist in Paris during the *Belle Epoque*: *flâniking* (flâneuring while hiking), and *flâmotoring* (flâneuring while driving). We got pretty good at not planning too much, getting off the beaten path, and just following our noses. But I have to admit with a dollop of pride, these past few weeks in Northern Portugal I think that Teresa and I finally achieved *peak flâneur*.

After our friends Tom and Paula left us, we had about three weeks to go before our long journey back to the US. Our last night in Porto, we had nothing, literally *nothing* booked for the rest of the trip, and only the vaguest notions of where we wanted to go in the remote northern parts of Portugal. We took it one step at a time, never booking more than a few nights ahead at our next destination, so we could be free to extend the places we wanted to explore more fully.

Even our route we left undecided. Generally, we rely on the Apple map app—programmed with the voice of a delightfully optimistic-sounding Irish lass we call Mary Margaret, who mangles the pronunciation of Portuguese place names most horrendously. Unfortunately, Mary Margaret does not always offer the most interesting routes. So we also use an old-school paper map of Portugal with the "green roads" marked that show the scenic byways. Whenever there's a greener option, we take it, much to Mary Margaret's distress:

"At the roundabout, make a U-Turn!" she says in her cheerful Irish accent. Under her breath, we imagine we hear her curse— "*Jesus-Mary-and-Joseph! They missed the feckin' turn again!*"

Sometimes these digressions get us lost. "Lost" usually carries an unfortunately negative meaning, but that was not our experience. To us, "lost" has simply come to mean an unanticipated adventure.

Because we got "lost" we ended up driving up and down the labyrinthine streets of forgotten towns, where it's not easy to even find a café with a glass of *vinho verde*. These accidental detours took us to places where we discovered new facets of old Portugal: ancient monuments, ornately decorated churches, war memorials dedicated to sons who died in faraway lands, statues of heroes and poets immortalized in their humble hometowns.

Some places felt like home. Might we come back some time to stay a month or six? Yes, in Viana do Castello, with its rich history of local festivals and traditions. Not so much in Bragança, which was charming, had just as much history, but ultimately did not resonate as a place we might want to stay. In fact, this became a topic conversation: Could we live here? In this quiet beach resort? In this remote mountain village? In this walled city where every granite wall seeps with history?

Having lived most of our lives in cities, we discovered neither of us wants to spend our twilight years in urban landscapes. Both of us like wilderness and a certain sense of vastness— whether by the sea or the mountains. But we are not ready to live in complete isolation, either. We both want to be part of a community. It feels like we have many miles ahead of us before we settle down anywhere, but talking about it is something new for both of us, and perhaps it's appropriate for Mature Flanêurs to contemplate the final stop at the end of the road, someday.

Someday. But not today.

On reaching Portugal's eastern border with Spain, we resigned ourselves to continuing northeast into Galatia, through the Basque region, back into France and then on to Paris to catch our flight to the US. That would have been the logical thing to do. But, the day before we were due to leave, we couldn't do it. We just had not had enough of Portugal. Well, where else do we want to go, we asked ourselves? We had driven through every part of the north, so what was left?

I still wanted to see the paleolithic rock art of the Coa Valley. Teresa felt she did not get enough of the gorgeous vineyards of the Douro. We had time to do both. So we made the improbable decision to turn around and drive south and then west again. It was ridiculous. If you looked at our route on a map, it would resemble a poorly fashioned bow tie.

We ended up spending our final days at Quinta Ventozelo, a posh hotel operating on a vineyard estate in the Douro Valley, overlooking the town of Pinhão. On the terraced hills across the river, we could make out the houses of the little town where we stayed the previous month when we first arrived in northern Portugal. We had come full circle, back to the knot of the bow tie.

There was nothing really left for us to do. We had seen all the sights of the Douro first time through. So we strolled around the vineyard—the vines now denuded of grapes, leaves turning rusty red in the fall air. Olives ripened from green to black in the groves owned by the *quinta*. We enjoyed their aromatic herb garden and the many fruit-filled orange and lemon trees that dotted the property. We explored the old buildings, brightened by a new lick of white paint, where the wine was fermented and stored in giant oak vats.

These final days in the Douro satisfied that yearning we had for a little bit more of Portugal. Then, oh so reluctantly, we set our face towards Spain, France, and the USA. There will be responsibilities down the line, we know. Family to visit for Thanksgiving and Christmas. An election to vote in. Taxes to file.

But for the present moment, there is the open road, the next hotel. Longsuffering Mary Margaret awaits us in the car each morning. What road will we take on the long drive ahead? We do not really know. How can we predict the choices tomorrow's Teresa and Tim will make? We are not the boss of them. They will have their way; they will have their whim. For these two, they have achieved *peak flâneur*.

Mature flâneurs one year later, October 2022, by the Bay of Biscay.

Epilogue

Three Rs for Re-entry

Flâneur Lesson #16: Let your flâneuring change your life

My friend and fellow wanderer, Chris Humphreys, asked me a pertinent question: "Any advice about how to finally go home? Very ambivalent at the idea of stopping."

He and his partner, Cat, had spent 100 days traveling through Europe and were poised to return. Based on our experience, here's a bit of advice for Chris and other long-term travelers who find themselves homeward bound:

1. Reconnect

Reconnecting was the main reason we came back and spent the holiday season with our friends and relatives. Both Teresa and I have rich networks of relationships that we left behind. We were looking forward to seeing everyone again. But, I have to say that a few things surprised us.

We were amazed at how little curiosity most people had about our year abroad. Beyond the "so, how was it?" general question, not too many folks seemed all that interested in listening to us recount the many tales of our adventures. We were startled to realize that a lot of people don't like to travel, and so are not particularly interested in hearing stories about places they'll never visit.

Now, in the case of my friends who are readers of my blog, they already knew my best stories. Occasionally, I would launch in to something like encountering walruses on Svalbard, and they would cut me off with, "yeah, yeah, I know!" One close buddy told me, when we went for our first walk together, "Tim, so great to see you. I've been following your blog all year. Now, I'll talk about me…"

The reality is, people are embedded in their own lives, and our friendships are forged from our common experiences. So, when you are gone for several months or more, you are kind of a blank space that does not really need to be filled in for many people. The point is, don't be offended when friends don't want to hear your fascinating travel stories. That's not reconnecting for them.

2. Re-engage

When traveling, each day provides its own adventure. There's always something new, stimulating, challenging awaiting you. I think if you just plonk down and rest after a long journey, that can lead to boredom, dissatisfaction, maybe even depression. I knew if I just sat around, I would have focused on missing my adventures, rather than enjoying my present circumstances.

Fortunately, we planned our return just before the US election. I volunteered to canvass and poll watch, which was a great experience. (Actually, it was impressive to watch democracy at work in the US, and to see the seriousness with which local poll volunteers did their job.) In mid November, Teresa and I had a work assignment: a series of four webinars that lasted almost two weeks and put us in a work groove. Then it was Thanksgiving.

Re-engaging like this kept us busy and prevented us from falling into a funk.

3. Reflect

Reconnecting and re-engaging would have been an adequate strategy if our intention had simply been to take a vacation and then merge back into the lives we had left behind. But in fact, we really wanted our "senior gap year" to be more than that: this was a time for us to reassess where our lives are heading as our careers wind down, while we still feel too young to settle into full retirement. So it was important for us to process what the past year meant for us. Indeed, these conversations began before we even stepped on an airplane to return stateside.

One of the things that emerged for both of us was a strange feeling of dislocation. We recognized the year had changed us. We didn't actually fit back into our old lives, even if we had wanted that. It was strange that some of our friends, while happy to see us, were not particularly seeking us out, not changing plans already made to accommodate our limited visit. We realized their lives had moved forward without us. I suppose for some, they didn't really know how to fit us back into their rhythm.

We discovered we were okay with that. The dislocation seemed natural, because we ourselves felt incomplete with the past year. We had already discussed "year two" of wandering. Being "back," didn't feel like being home. We didn't know where home was any more. And maybe that was the success of year one: that it has led us to wanting year two. What we seem to have accomplished in our first year of flâneuring is creating a clearing in our lives. A blank page that feels good to both of us. We don't want go back to a previous chapter, nor are we ready to start writing a new one.

One of the most amazing things about travel is the new perspective it provides. So take the time to reflect when your flâneuring is done. You had the courage to change your life when you departed, so use that courage to change your life when you return.

If you want to join Teresa and me on our travels, you are welcome to follow my travel blog on Medium.com at: timward-changermakers.medium.com.

Appendix

Flâneur Lessons

Flâneur lesson #1: Surprise yourself—Ch 2

Flâneur lesson #2: Let go of work—Ch 4

Flâneur lesson #3: Put away your phone—Ch 5

Flâneur lesson #4: Open your eyes—Ch 6

Flâneur lesson #5: You can time travel—Ch 10

Flâneur lesson #6: Walk without a destination—Ch 11

Flâneur lesson # 7: Find art everywhere—Ch 13

Flâneur Lesson #8: Pursue the unexpected—Ch 14

Flâneur lesson #9: Yield to the whim—Ch 15

Flâneur lesson #10: Do one thing at a time—Ch 18

Flâneur lesson #11: Flâneuring while hiking = flâniking—Ch 22

Flâneur lesson #12: Flâmotoring is also a thing—Ch 23

Flâneur lesson #13: Embrace the awe—Ch 30

Flâneur lesson #14: The edge is everywhere—Ch 39

Flâneur lesson #15: Don't believe the brochure—Ch 52

Flâneur lesson #16: Let your flâneuring change your life—Epilogue

**CHANGEMAKERS
BOOKS**

Transform your life, transform our world. Changemakers Books publishes books for people who seek to become positive, powerful agents of change. These books inform, inspire, and provide practical wisdom and skills to empower us to write the next chapter of humanity's future.

www.changemakers-books.com

Other Literary Travel Books by Tim Ward

Zombies on Kilimanjaro
A Father/Son Journey Above the Clouds
On a journey to the roof of Africa, a father and son traverse the treacherous terrain of fatherhood, divorce, dark secrets and old grudges, and forge an authentic new relationship.

Savage Breast
One Man's Search for the Goddess
We think of God as male, but the most common representation of the divine through our history has been the Goddess. When did this major change happen, and why? Tim Ward went on an epic search through the ruins of ancient Europe to find the answers. What he discovered changed his life—and his relationship with women.

What the Buddha Never Taught
20th Anniversary Edition
A humorous behind-the-robes account of life in a Thai forest monastery. A cult classic.

Current Bestsellers from Changemakers Books

Resetting our Future: Am I Too Old to Save the Planet?
A Boomer's Guide to Climate Action
Lawrence MacDonald

Why American boomers are uniquely responsible for the
climate crisis — and what to do about it.

Resetting our Future: Feeding Each Other Shaping Change in
Food Systems through Relationship Michelle
Auerbach and Nicole Civita
Our collective survival depends on making food systems more
relational; this guidebook for shaping change in food systems
offers a way to find both security and pleasure in a more
connected, well-nourished life.

Resetting Our Future: Zero Waste Living, The 80/20 Way
The Busy Person's Guide to a Lighter Footprint
Stephanie J. Miller
Empowering the busy individual to do the easy things that
have a real impact on the climate and waste crises.

The Way of the Rabbit
Mark Hawthorne
An immersion in the world of rabbits: their habitats, evolution
and biology; their role in legend, literature, and popular
culture; and their significance as household companions.